eight sessions for
a children's club

© Scripture Union 2004
First published 2004

ISBN 1 85999 767 8

Scripture Union, 207–209 Queensway, Bletchley, Milton Keynes, MK2 2EB, United Kingdom
Email: info@scriptureunion.org.uk
Website: www.scriptureunion.org.uk

Scripture Union Australia, Locked Bag 2, Central Coast Business Centre, NSW 2252, Australia
Website: www.su.org.au

Scripture Union USA, PO Box 987, Valley Forge, PA 19482
Website: www.scriptureunion.org

Scripture quotations are from the Contemporary English Version © American Bible Society 1991, 1992, 1995. Anglicisations © British and Foreign Bible Society 1997, published in the UK by HarperCollins*Publishers*. Used by permission.

British Library Cataloguing-in-Publication Data.
A catalogue record of this book is available from the British Library.

Printed and bound in Malta by Interprint.
Cover and internal design by Kevin Wade of kwgraphicdesign.

Special thanks to the following clubs who took part in the **Streetwise** trial:
Jam Club at Evesham Baptist Church; **King's Club**, Kendal Road Baptist Church, Gloucester; **Re:Fresh**, Cotton End Baptist Church, Bedford; **Focus**, Barrow Baptist Church, Loughborough; **(H)our Club**, Christ the Rock Christian Fellowship, Yate; **Heversham CE School**, Kendal; **Chattabox**, St Laurence Church, Measham; **4th Newtonabbey Boys Brigade**, Carnomney Presbyterian Church, Newtonabbey; **1st Wokingham Girls Brigade**, Wokingham Baptist Church; **17th Nottingham Boys Brigade and 30th Girls Brigade**, The Pearson Centre for Young People, Beeston; **1st Ketley Boys Brigade**, Shropshire; **Storykeepers**, North Cheam Baptist Church, Cheam.

Thanks also to Sue Clutterham, Helen Franklin and Steve Hutchinson for their input.

Scripture Union is an international Christian charity working with churches in more than 130 countries, providing resources to bring the good news of Jesus Christ to children, young people and families and to encourage them to develop spiritually through the Bible and prayer.

As well as our network of volunteers, staff and associates who run holidays, church-based events and school Christian groups, we produce a wide range of publications and support those who use our resources through training programmes.

**This book is dedicated to all the groups
who took part in the Streetwise trial**

Contents

STARTING OUT

How to use Streetwise

Be Streetwise!

Come on a journey down Luke Street! Visit houses mentioned in Luke's Gospel to find out why Jesus went there and what happened when he did! Meet Zacchaeus, Jairus and his daughter, Peter's mother-in-law and Martha and Mary (but avoid the kitchen). Find out about expensive perfume and expensive holes in the roof. But most of all, learn about the power and authority of Jesus as he meets with these people and changes their lives.

The aim of Streetwise

The aim is to help everyone meet Jesus, who can change *their* lives too. The activities make very few assumptions about children's previous knowledge of the Bible, so they are suitable for children who don't have any church background. There is plenty of scope for relationship building – with each other and with God.

At the heart of **Streetwise** is the intention that children have fun as they build relationships with other children and adult leaders. In this context, leaders can naturally share Jesus and what he means to them. Over the weeks, trust will grow, as will the questions children ask and the answers they find. Our hope is that the Holy Spirit will be at work in the life of each child who attends, whether this is the first time they have been part of anything Christian or they are already part of a church community.

How the programme works

This menu-style material is designed to go with the **Streetwise** DVD – eight four-minute cartoon stories – one for each of the eight **Streetwise** sessions.

The DVD can be used with or without Roy Castle's introduction. In the trial, many leaders found the introductions to the cartoon stories were off-putting due to the age of the original recording. However, they went down really well with the children.

Several children commented that the stories weren't long enough!
Becky, Bedford

Children are still entranced by Roy Castle's introductions and personality. So decide what is best for your group.

Thirteen midweek clubs tested the **Streetwise** programme before publication. Comments from these trials shaped the published programme. Some comments have been printed for your inspiration!

> If you don't have access to a DVD player, the material is also available in video format as the *Luke Street* video. This is available from SU Mail Order or from your local Christian bookshop.

The **Streetwise** song, on page 26, was specially written for the club. It is available on the CD *Light for Everyone* (£9.99, 1 84427 080 7, SCRIPTCD01), which also contains non-confessional songs ideal for use if you have children not connected to the church in your group. *Light for Everyone* also contains a CD-ROM of song words and sheet music. The **Streetwise** song is also available on the **Streetwise** DVD.

Each session of **Streetwise** is divided into three parts – Open the door, Step inside and Make yourself at home. Choose some or all of the activities on offer in each part. The times in brackets for each activity give an indication of the time the activity might take. Choose as many activities as you need for the time you have.

- The activities that would work well with older children are marked with 😊.
- Activities that are especially appropriate for small groups are marked with ✣.

You will soon discover what goes down well with your group.

Part 1: Open the door
(5–20 minutes)

Open the door is a selection of fun activities that introduce the session's theme. They involve movement, games and action – a good way for everyone to get to enjoy being together and let off steam at the beginning of a session. Vary the time according to the mood of the children as they arrive, the type of venue you have, the number of helpers and the time available for your session.

If your group is meeting straight after school, the children may need to run around and let off steam or they may be tired out. They will certainly need refreshments. After their evening meal, they will be more relaxed. On Saturday or Sunday they will be different again. You will have to assess what best introduces them to the **Streetwise** atmosphere. However, don't make the mistake of allowing this part of the programme to go on too long. Allow enough time for *Step inside* and *Make yourself at home.*

Ideas for those first five minutes, and any other time you might have a bit of extra time, are on page 14. Whatever you do, make sure that the children feel properly welcomed and are comfortable.

Part 2: Step inside
(10 minutes)

Step inside focuses on each session's theme in detail, using the Bible verses and the video. Do 'See the film' (the **Streetwise** DVD) and 'Read the book' (the Bible verses), maybe including the drama option, if you have people willing to take part. A range of activities in *Make yourself at home* develop the theme.

Remember that some children find reading hard or just don't like it. Reading the Bible may appear hard work and very foreign: but it doesn't have to be! Children can listen to it

being read, they can act it out, draw it, memorise it, set it to music, pick out key words and so on. Bible reading is deliberately central to this programme. That is why the Bible passages are included, so you can put them on an acetate if you want to. The Bible could be part of a child's life, long after you have left them! So be imaginative in how you use it. Your enthusiasm for God's word will be infectious.

The Bible verses have been reproduced from the Contemporary English Version and used with permission. This version is especially good for reading out loud. But whatever version of the Bible you use, make sure it is child-friendly and not tatty!

Part 3: Make yourself at home
(15–60 minutes)

Make yourself at home suggests activities to consolidate the learning. Select activities according to the size of the group, the ages of the children and the help you have available.

Make sure that you end properly and as calmly as possible. Try to say goodbye to each child personally. The children will be more likely then to remember what they have learnt and be aware of the positive relationships there have been in **Streetwise**. Friendships made with other children and the leaders may be the most memorable part of **Streetwise**.

Catch up with other **Streetwise** users on the **Streetwise** website! Exchange ideas on the bulletin board, check out the drama ideas for each day and download PDFs of the photocopiable pages:
www.scriptureunion.org.uk/streetwise

Where you see this symbol, these features are available on the website.

Getting to know you...

⊕ Building relationships

The children you'll meet at **Streetwise** live in a fast-moving, sophisticated, technology-orientated world, dominated by screens. There is so much 'stuff' demanding their attention. Rather than trying to compete with that sort of environment, offer them what they are missing elsewhere – real communication. Concentrate on the unique opportunity you have to build relationships, to listen to them, talk with them, and give them time as you show them God's love in action. That way they will get to know you, each other and Jesus on their journey down Luke Street, and have a great time while they are doing it!

⊕ Top tips for sharing Jesus with children

- **Build strong friendships.** Be genuinely interested in their lives, homes, interests, what happens at school. These friendships will be bridges across which Jesus can walk! Ensure that these children know that you appreciate and respect them.
- **Be informed** about what is happening at school and home – it's useful to be in the know about sports days, class excursions or family events and these may explain why the children are excited or tired, or both!
- **Get to know the children's families:** understand their home lives, and help their parents (or whoever is responsible for their care) know what they are learning. Children can never be divorced from their home backgrounds .Avoid talking about Mum and Dad. It's best to refer to Mum *or* Dad or even, 'whoever looks after you at home'.
- **Remember birthdays,** or ask someone else to take on the responsibility of noting dates and preparing cards, perhaps for the other children to sign.
- **Do as you say!** The children need to see you model what you teach them. Your friendship with Jesus matters. How else will the children see what it means in practice to be in a relationship with him?

- **Encourage everyone to join in** – adults and children alike. Create a 'we're in this together' feel to the sessions, rather than 'them and us' – avoid organising activities that adults stand and watch. Relax, have fun and learn with the children – '…aim to give children the best hour of their week!' (Dave Connelly, Frontline Church)
- **Mind your language!** Avoid jargon words (eg sin, grace or churchy words) and explain what you mean by things like prayer.
- **Use illustrations from everyday life** to explain concepts. Jesus taught complex truths in simple ways (eg you can't see wind, but you can see the effects that it has; it's the same with the Holy Spirit). You will need to think about this before the club begins.
- **Grow confidence with the Bible** and explain how to read it. Why don't we often start at page 1? How do we use the contents page? (Younger children find this very hard.) What are the differences between chapters and verses, or the Old and New Testaments? How do you explain that the Bible is one big story – God's story – in different bits?
- **Talk about Jesus,** rather than God, where possible. The Gospels give us clear pictures of what he is like and these are far easier to grasp than the idea of God being 'up there' but invisible. Children have some very woolly ideas about God, but there is less room for manoeuvre when it comes to Jesus!
- **Apply the Bible teaching appropriately:** 'If Jesus came to your house, like he went to tea with Zacchaeus, what do you think he would say and do?' Help them see that Jesus is alive today and is relevant to their lives.
- **Allow children to make responses** that are appropriate for them, their understanding and their backgrounds. Don't rush straight in with, 'Do you want to follow Jesus?' That should be a decision that lasts for life, and they need to recognise what it entails. For many children, there are a number of commitments as their understanding grows.
- **Have fun together!** The children need to catch something of the 'life in all its fullness' that Jesus spoke about.

Working with small groups

⊕ Practicalities

- Children are all different. Respect their differences.
- Make sure any child with a special need is catered for.
- Make sure children know they can come to you with any questions.
- Make sure that children are comfortable. Cold, hard floors do not encourage positive discussion. Cushions, mats or comfortable chairs can make all the difference. Sometimes, everyone lying on their tummies in a star shape can create a fantastic atmosphere – their teacher at school is unlikely to do this.
- Keep good eye contact with every child.
- In the group, watch out for children who are on the edge.
- Don't talk down to children – talk with them. This means getting to their level, physically and verbally.
- Don't always rush to fill silences while children are thinking of responses.
- Validate all responses, either by a further question or ask others what they think, especially if you don't agree with the initial comment or answer.
- If lots of children want to talk, pass an object round – only the child holding the object can speak.
- Encourage children to listen to each other (something they might find quite difficult).
- Be prepared to admit that you don't know the answer to a question, but say that you'll find out the answer, if appropriate.

⊕ Asking questions

In each session, there is a section on questions that you might ask in any group time you have, which will help the children to engage with the Bible story. Leading a small group is one of the most difficult things a children's worker has to do. Don't use all these questions as they are written. Put them into your own words. They are simply a guide for you. The questions have sometimes been incorporated into a quiz.

Ever thought about the kinds of questions you ask people? The same question can be asked in many different ways, and force the person being asked the question to give certain kinds of answers.

?? Rhetorical

If you ask, 'Isn't it great to have ice cream?', it is a **rhetorical question**, implying the expected answer. It brings out the right answer for the benefit of others.

?? Closed

If you ask, 'Do you like coming to **Streetwise**?', it is a **closed question**, mainly allowing for 'Yes' or 'No'. It encourages contributions and assesses what the children think.

?? Factual

If you ask, 'What did Zacchaeus climb?', it is a **factual question**, requiring basic information. It encourages contributions and establishes the facts.

?? Open

If you ask, 'Why did Jesus go to Zacchaeus' house?', it is an **open question**, allowing broad expression. It encourages discussion and indicates what the children think.

?? Experience

If you ask, 'How would you feel if that happened to you?', it is an **experience question**, for sharing views or feelings. It encourages discussion and helps children to apply the teaching personally.

?? Leading

If you ask, 'What have you learnt at **Streetwise**, David?', it is a **leading question** aimed at getting a specific answer from someone. It indicates learning and understanding and encourages contributions.

Think about when you might use these questions in your group. Go through each question with your team and decide when it is appropriate and when it is inappropriate to use certain kinds of questions.

Helping children to respond

Friends with Jesus

Streetwise introduces children to people in Luke Street who met Jesus and got to know him. They'll also meet people in the 21st century who know and love Jesus. This may prompt children to want to be friends with Jesus for themselves. Be ready to help them.

- They rarely need long explanations, just simple answers to questions.
- Talk to them in a place where you can be seen by others.
- Never put pressure on children to respond in a particular way, just help them take one step closer to Jesus when they are ready. We don't want them to respond just to please us!
- Remember, for many children there are a number of commitments as their understanding grows.
- Many children just need a bit of help to say what they want to say to God. Here is a suggested prayer they could use to make a commitment to Jesus:

> Dear Father God,
> Thank you that you love me.
> I'm sorry for all the things I have done wrong, which you do not want me to do.
> Thank you that Jesus your Son came to live on earth and understands what it's like.
> Thank you that he died on the cross for me and that means I can be forgiven.
> Please forgive me.
> Please be my friend and help me each day to please you.
> Amen.

Reassure them that God hears us when we talk with him and has promised to forgive us and help us be his friends.

What next?

Children need help to stick with Jesus, especially if their parents don't believe.

- Assure them that God wants to hear whatever they say. Give them some prayer ideas.
- Encourage them to keep coming to Christian activities, not necessarily on Sundays – their church might have to be the midweek club or a school lunch-time club.
- Reading the Bible will be easier with something like *Snapshots* – but you need to support them if they are to keep it up.
- Keep praying and maintain your relationship with them wherever possible.

Some booklets that may help

Want to be in God's family?
P Butler
1 85999 256 0 (25-pack)
£18.75
1 85999 245 5 (single) £0.75

Growing up in God's family
P Butler
1 85999 246 3 (single) £0.99
1 85999 252 8 (10-pack)
£9.90

Would you like to know Jesus?
G Jefferson and E Reeves
0 86201 577 4 £0.65
(For younger children.)

What Jesus did
D Abrahall
1 84427 005 X (single) £0.99
1 84427 006 8 (5-pack)
£5.00
(For those with special needs.)

Snapshots
Bible reading for
8- to 11-year-olds
£2.50 single copy
£9.00 annual subscription
(Six-packs are also available.)

What to do after Streetwise

Step one – time to think

Hopefully **Streetwise** has made you think about how you run activities and reach out to children in your community. Before the end of the **Streetwise** series, plan a review with anyone who helped. Be as honest as you can and dream dreams!

- What did the children enjoy about **Streetwise**?
- What was different compared to your previous activities for children?
- Were there more small-group activities? How did they work?
- Was there more Bible input than before?
- What worked really well or didn't work?
- What did the leaders enjoy?
- What did you discover about each other's gifts for working with children? Was there an unknown storyteller or someone especially good at welcoming children?

Write down the most important answers. Talk about what you should do next.

Step two – moving on

Don't be afraid to develop what you provide for children. If **Streetwise** encouraged you to run a midweek or Saturday club for the first time and it worked, plan to carry on. You may need extra help, especially if some people can't commit themselves weekly. Perhaps you could do another eight-week club next term or maybe a monthly Saturday/Sunday special, using another Scripture Union programme.

Discuss how you might contact new children. What are your links with the local school(s) or neighbourhood groups? Could you publicise your group through the local paper or library? How could the children who already come be encouraged to bring their friends? Just how many more children can you cope with?

One club for 5- to 9-year-olds had a special 'Bring a friend' evening. They got so enthusiastic that mums in the playground had to sort out who was bringing whom, to stop fights breaking out!
Steve, Gloucester

Step three – building on Streetwise

One of the aims of **Streetwise** is to bring children who don't usually come into a Christian activity. If this worked for you, build on the final **Streetwise** session and get to know the children's families by running a parents' special event. Family games work well, either games to play as families or everyone all together. Any family activity that offers food will be popular! Alternatively, some churches have explored parenting groups – in one place, a church football team has developed from fathers of children who started coming to a church children's club. Be imaginative and find out what other churches have done in your area. Maybe you could do something together.

Coming soon

Look out for Awesome!, another eight-session midweek club programme from Scripture Union. Based on the signs of Jesus in John's Gospel, the programme is accompanied by a video. Like Streetwise, Awesome! is designed specifically for use with children who have little or no contact with church or Christianity.

Extra activities

The first and last few minutes of a club can be the most important! Your first conversation with a child helps to settle them, for them to be open to God. You represent Jesus: your welcome is his welcome. The end of the club may be what they remember most, so make the most of the time.

A few guidelines

- Choose the right one for the right day: if it's the weekend, keep school conversation to a minimum.
- Be led by the child. Don't probe where they don't want to talk.
- Allow a conversation to develop rather than just asking questions.
- Help others join in as they join the group.
- Tell the children about your day to build friendships and make it less like a grilling.

Questions about school

What was the best thing that happened? Did anything funny happen? What did you have for dinner? What's the food like at your school?

General questions

What have you seen on television/read/done recently? What are you doing this weekend? How's your football team doing? Tell me a bit about your family/pets/what you do in your spare time.

Ideas to end the club

A routine pattern to the end may be useful.

In groups

- Chat about what they will do at home/later/ during the week.
- A quick recap of the Bible teaching to help them remember/apply it.
- Write or draw on the back of each child's **Streetwise** pass what they remember.
- Pray for the week ahead.

Together

- Recap the Bible teaching and allow a moment to think about it again.
- Sit around a lit candle and remind them that Jesus, the light of the world, is always with us. Ask for things to pray about, or read prayers they have written during the session.
- Sing the **Streetwise** song at the end of each session.

Time-fillers

1 Turn everyone's name round and enjoy the different sounds! (Nhoj Htims, Enna Senoj)

2 I Spy. For very young children play 'I spy with my colour eye', looking for objects of a certain colour.

3 Who can… wiggle their ears, touch their nose with their tongue, recite the alphabet backwards, wiggle their eyebrows and so on.

4 Dice games: have ready-made cards with questions to be answered when the numbers are rolled.
For example:
Favourites: 1 – food; 2 – pop group; 3 – team; 4 – TV programme; 5 – story; 6 – colour
Home: 1 – family; 2 – rooms; 3 – pets; 4 – food; 5 – outside the house; 6 – favourite room
Favourite food: 1 – sandwich; 2 – drink; 3 – breakfast; 4 – biscuits; 5 – snack; 6 – worst food

5 Simon Says: 'Simon says, "Walk down Luke Street".' etc.

6 'I walked down Luke Street and I saw a…' Each person recites the growing list and adds an item.

7 Mime things you do at home – others must guess, eg watching TV, turning on a tap, cleaning teeth.

8 Challenge the group to make a human sculpture of household objects, eg a chair, knife and fork, clock, bathroom.

The book of Luke

These Bible verses for **Streetwise** are taken from the Contemporary English Version and used with permission.

Pages 15 to 27 are photocopiable. You may photocopy any of these pages for use in your **Streetwise** programme. These pages are also available on the **Streetwise** website: www.scriptureunion.org.uk/streetwise

---

 ### Session 1: The Sick House

Luke 4:38–40

Jesus left the meeting place and went to Simon's home. When Jesus got there, he was told that Simon's mother-in-law was sick with a high fever. So Jesus went over to her and ordered the fever to go away. At once she was able to get up and serve them a meal.

After the sun had set, people with all kinds of diseases were brought to Jesus. He put his hands on each one of them and healed them.

 ### Session 2: The Crowded House

Luke 5:17–26

God had given Jesus the power to heal the sick, and some people came carrying a crippled man on a mat. They tried to take him inside the house and put him in front of Jesus. But because of the crowd, they could not get him to Jesus. So they went up on the roof, where they removed some tiles and let the mat down in the middle of the room.

When Jesus saw how much faith they had, he said to the crippled man, "My friend, your sins are forgiven."

The Pharisees and the experts began arguing, "Jesus must think he is God! Only God can forgive sins."

Jesus knew what they were thinking, and he said, "Why are you thinking that? Is it easier for me to tell this crippled man that his sins are forgiven or to tell him to get up and walk? But now you will see that the Son of Man has the right to forgive sins here on earth." Jesus then said to the man, "Get up! Pick up your mat and walk home."

At once the man stood up in front of everyone. He picked up his mat and went home, giving thanks to God. Everyone was amazed and praised God. What they saw surprised them, and they said, "We've seen a great miracle today!"

Session 3: The Rich House

Luke 7:36–40,44–50

A Pharisee invited Jesus to have dinner with him. So Jesus went to the Pharisee's home and got ready to eat.

When a sinful woman in that town found out that Jesus was there, she bought an expensive bottle of perfume. Then she came and stood behind Jesus. She cried and started washing his feet with her tears and drying them with her hair. The woman kissed his feet and poured the perfume on them.

The Pharisee who had invited Jesus saw this and said to himself, "If this man really were prophet, he would know what kind of woman is touching him! He would know that she is a sinner!"

Jesus said to the Pharisee, "Simon, I have something to say to you."

"Teacher, what is it?" Simon replied.

He turned towards the woman and said to Simon, "Have you noticed this woman? When I came into your home, you didn't give me any water so I could wash my feet. But she has washed my feet with her tears and dried them with her hair. You didn't greet me with a kiss, but from the time I came in, she has not stopped kissing my feet. You didn't even pour olive oil on my head, but she has poured expensive perfume on my feet. So I tell you that all her sins are forgiven, and that is why she has shown great love. But anyone who has been forgiven for only a little will show only a little love."

Then Jesus said to the woman, "Your sins are forgiven."

Some other guests started saying to one another, "Who is this who dares to forgive sins?"

But Jesus told the woman, "Because of your faith, you are now saved. May God give you peace!"

Session 4: The Leader's House

Luke 8:40–42,49–56

Everyone had been waiting for Jesus, and when he came back, a crowd was there to welcome him. Just then the man in charge of the Jewish meeting place came and knelt down in front of Jesus. His name was Jairus, and he begged Jesus to come to his home because his 12-year-old child was dying. She was his only daughter.

Someone came from Jairus' home and said, "Your daughter has died! Why bother the teacher any more?"

When Jesus heard this, he told Jairus, "Don't worry! Have faith, and your daughter will get well."

Jesus went into the house, but he did not let anyone else go in with him, except Peter, John, James, and the girl's father and mother. Everyone was crying and weeping for the girl. But Jesus said, "The child isn't dead. She is just asleep." The people laughed at him because they knew she was dead.

Jesus took hold of the girl's hand and said, "Child, get up!" She came back to life and got straight up. Jesus told them to give her something to eat. Her parents were surprised, but Jesus ordered them not to tell anyone what had happened.

Session 5: The Guest House

Luke 10:38–42

The Lord and his disciples were travelling along and came to a village. When they got there, a woman named Martha welcomed him into her home. She had a sister named Mary, who sat down in front of the Lord and was listening to what he said. Martha was worried about all that had to be done.

Finally, she went to Jesus and said, "Lord, doesn't it bother you that my sister has left me to do all the work by myself? Tell her to come and help me!"

The Lord answered, "Martha, Martha! You are worried and upset about so many things, but only one thing is necessary. Mary has chosen what is best, and it will not be taken away from her."

Session 6: The Cheat's House

Luke 19:1–10

Jesus was going through Jericho, where a man named Zacchaeus lived. He was in charge of collecting taxes and was very rich. Jesus was heading his way, and Zacchaeus wanted to see what he was like. But Zacchaeus was a short man and could not see over the crowd. So he ran ahead and climbed up into a sycamore tree.

When Jesus got there, he looked up and said, "Zacchaeus, hurry down! I want to stay with you today." Zacchaeus hurried down and gladly welcomed Jesus.

Everyone who saw this started grumbling, "This man Zacchaeus is a sinner! And Jesus is going home to eat with him."

Later that day Zacchaeus stood up and said to the Lord, 'I will give half of my property to the poor. And I will now pay back four times as much to everyone I have ever cheated."

Jesus said to Zacchaeus, "Today you and your family have been saved, because you are a true son of Abraham. The Son of Man came to look for and to save people who are lost."

Session 7: The Secret House

Luke 22:8–13,19,20; 23:33,34,46; 24:1–6

Jesus said to Peter and John, "Go and prepare the Passover meal for us to eat."

But they asked, "Where do you want us to prepare it?"

Jesus told them, "As you go into the city, you will meet a man carrying a jar of water. Follow him into the house and say to the owner, 'Our teacher wants to know where he can eat the Passover meal with his disciples.' The owner will take you upstairs and show you a large room ready for you to use. Prepare the meal there."

Peter and John left. They found everything just as Jesus had told them, and they prepared the Passover meal.

Jesus took some bread in his hands and gave thanks for it. He broke the bread and handed it to his apostles. Then he said, "This is my body, which is given for you. Eat this as a way of remembering me!"

After the meal he took another cup of wine in his hands. Then he said, "This is my blood. It is poured out for you, and with it God makes his new agreement."

The soldiers … nailed Jesus to a cross … Jesus said, "Father, forgive these people! They don't know what they're doing."

Jesus shouted, "Father, I put myself in your hands!" Then he died.

Very early on Sunday morning the women went to the tomb, carrying the spices that they had prepared. When they found the stone rolled away from the entrance, they went in. But they did not find the body of the Lord Jesus, and they did not know what to think.

Suddenly two men in shining white clothes stood beside them. The women were afraid and bowed to the ground. But the men said, "Why are you looking in the place of the dead for someone who is alive? Jesus isn't here! He has been raised from death."

Session 8: The Country House

Luke 24:13–43

That same day two of Jesus' disciples were going to the village of Emmaus, which was about 11 kilometres from Jerusalem. As they were talking and thinking about what had happened, Jesus came near and started walking along beside them. But they did not know who he was.

Jesus asked them, "What were you talking about as you walked along?"

The two of them stood there looking sad and gloomy. Then the one named Cleopas asked Jesus, "Are you the only person from Jerusalem who didn't know what was happening there these last few days?"

"What do you mean?" Jesus asked. They answered:

Those things that happened to Jesus from Nazareth. By what he did and said he showed that he was a powerful prophet, who pleased God and all the people. Then the chief priests and our leaders had him arrested and sentenced to die on a cross. We had hoped that he would be the one to set Israel free! But it has already been three days since all this happened.

Some women in our group surprised us. They had gone to the tomb early in the morning, but did not find the body of Jesus. They came back, saying that they had seen a vision of angels who told them that he is alive. Some men from our group went to the tomb and found it just as the women had said. But they didn't see Jesus either.

Then Jesus asked the two disciples, "Why can't you understand? How can you be so slow to believe all that the prophets said? Didn't you know that the Messiah would have to suffer before he was given his glory?" Jesus then explained everything written about himself in the Scriptures, beginning with the Law of Moses and the Books of the Prophets.

When the two of them came near the village where they were going, Jesus seemed to be going further. They begged him, "Stay with us! It's already late and the sun is going down." So Jesus went into the house to stay with them.

After Jesus sat down to eat, he took some bread. He blessed it and broke it. Then he gave it to them. At once they knew who he was, but he disappeared. They said to each other, "When he talked with us along the road and explained the Scriptures, didn't it warm our hearts?" So they got up at once and returned to Jerusalem.

The two disciples found the eleven apostles and the others gathered together. And they learnt from the group that the Lord was really alive and had appeared to Peter. Then the disciples from Emmaus told what happened on the road and how they knew he was the Lord when he broke the bread.

While Jesus' disciples were talking about what had happened, Jesus appeared and greeted them. They were frightened and terrified because they thought they were seeing a ghost.

But Jesus said, "Why are you so frightened? Why do you doubt? Look at my hands and my feet and see who I am! Touch me and find out for yourselves. Ghosts don't have flesh and bones as you see I have."

After Jesus said this, he showed them his hands and his feet. The disciples were so glad and amazed that they could not believe it. Jesus then asked them, "Do you have something to eat?" They gave him a piece of baked fish. He took it and ate it as they watched.

Luke Street

STREETWISE PASS

Name: _____
Address: _____
_____
_____
Signature

THE SICK HOUSE	THE CROWDED HOUSE
1 Stamp here	2 Stamp here
THE RICH HOUSE	THE LEADER'S HOUSE
3 Stamp here	4 Stamp here
THE GUEST HOUSE	THE CHEAT'S HOUSE
5 Stamp here	6 Stamp here
THE SECRET HOUSE	THE COUNTRY HOUSE
7 Stamp here	8 Stamp here

STREETWISE PASS

Name: _____
Address: _____
_____
_____
Signature

THE SICK HOUSE	THE CROWDED HOUSE
1 Stamp here	2 Stamp here
THE RICH HOUSE	THE LEADER'S HOUSE
3 Stamp here	4 Stamp here
THE GUEST HOUSE	THE CHEAT'S HOUSE
5 Stamp here	6 Stamp here
THE SECRET HOUSE	THE COUNTRY HOUSE
7 Stamp here	8 Stamp here

Crowded House

Sick House

Country House

Rich House

Guest House

Secret House

Cheat's House

Leader's House

1 Does anybody you know wear perfume? Do you like the smell?
2 Are you afraid of getting into trouble when you do something wrong?
3 When was the last time you were in trouble? What happened?
4 Do you ever cry when you have done something wrong? Why do you think you cry?
5 Have you ever owned up to something you have done, even when you had not been found out? Could you say why?
6 Sometimes at school or in families, some people are thought of as 'good' or 'bad'. Which would you want people to think of you?
7 Does it sometimes feel as if grown-ups want you to be good and other children think it's more exciting to be bad? What do you think?
8 What sort of things would you find difficult to forgive? (Check out Luke 6:37.)
9 How can we show Jesus we love him if we can't see him?
10 The woman's tears showed she was sorry. Check out 1 John 1:8,9. Do you think you can be forgiven if you aren't sorry?

Use with Session 3: The Rich House

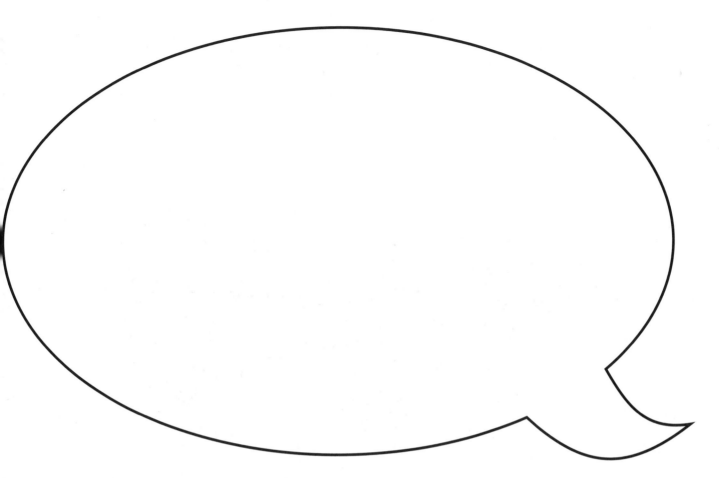

Use with Session 6: The Cheat's House

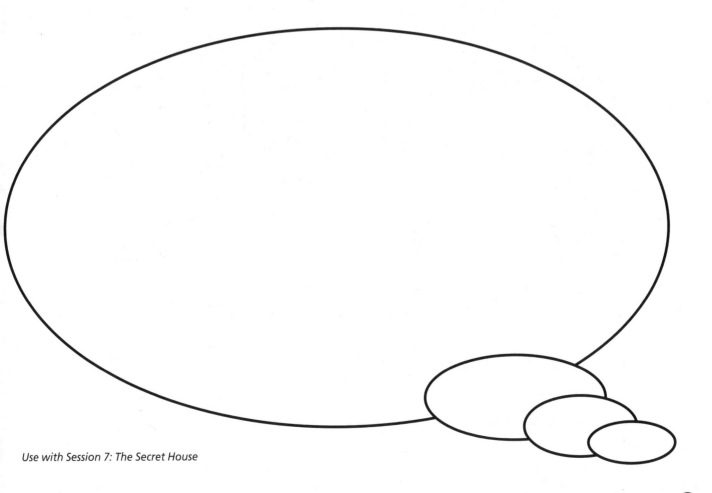

Use with Session 7: The Secret House

Use with Session 8: The Country House

Evaluation form

Use this evaluation form to review each session of Streetwise. Be open and honest about how you felt it went and include any suggestions you have for the next session. Adjust the material on the basis of what you decide here.

Aim

Did the session achieve the aim?

Open the door

How well did the *Open the door* activities you used relax the children and help them get into the story for this session?

What wouldn't you do again?

Step inside

How did the group respond to the way you presented the story? Were they able to engage with it? What did the children gain from the style of retelling you chose? How did they respond to the story?

Make yourself at home

How well did the activities you chose continue the theme of the session's story?

What wouldn't you do again?

The children

Which parts of the programme did the children react best to? Why do you think this was?

Think of each child. How did each child respond to the teaching? Is there any help you need to give to a specific child?

You

Identify any areas of the programme that you were unhappy with. What problems did you see and what solutions can you offer to the rest of your team? Do you have any other general comments?

Streetwise

Dave Godfrey

Steady rock ♩ = 130

1. On the streets of Ga - li - lee,__ Peo - ple were__ a - mazed to see,__ deaf hear,__ lame dance, Dead brought to life! On the streets of Ju - de - a,__ Peo - ple were__ a - mazed to hear,__ Sto - ries of__ their God a - bove, Sto - ries of__ a - maz - ing love!__ Je - sus is the street - wise King,__ On the streets they fol - lowed him.__ You could hear the peo - ple sing,__ 'Je - sus is__ the street - wise King!'

2. On the streets of Jericho,
People were amazed to know,
Bad, good, young, old,
Jesus loves them all.
On a hill in Jerusalem,
Jesus died for them,
People said, 'What have we done?
To the streetwise holy one!'

Photocopiable page

On the streets of Galilee,
People were amazed to see,
Deaf hear, lame dance,
Dead brought to life!
On the streets of Judea,
People were amazed to hear,
Stories of their God above,
Stories of amazing love!

Jesus is the streetwise King,
On the street they followed him.
You could hear the people sing,
Jesus is the streetwise King!
(Repeat.)

On the streets of Jericho,
People were amazed to know,
Bad, good, young, old,
Jesus loves them all.
On a hill in Jerusalem,
Jesus died for them,
People said, 'What have we done?
To the streetwise holy one!'

CCLI licence number _____

THE SICK HOUSE

Open the door

Welcome the children to Streetwise. Introduce yourself and any other adult helpers. Do the first activity, as it is a useful way of registering the children and obtaining contact details. Keep the passes in alphabetical order and date stamp each child's pass as they arrive at each session. For an extra touch, you could place the passes in see-through plastic pouches and the children could wear them as badges. Make sure the adult helpers wear passes too.

◖◗1 Streetwise visitor's pass
⊞ *(5 minutes)*

What you need
- A **Streetwise** pass for each person (photocopied from page 20 onto thin card)
- A pen for each person
- Date stamp and ink pad

What you do
Indicate the Luke Street sign. Explain that each session everyone will be taking a journey down Luke Street, stopping at different houses that Jesus visited. To do this, they will need a **Streetwise** pass. Distribute the passes and pens and allow a few minutes for the adult helpers and children to complete them. They should fill in the details on the card and draw their picture in the space. Ask the children to write one or two interesting facts about themselves on the back of the picture section of their pass, eg what their favourite food is or which football team they support.

When the children have completed their passes, either with help or on their own, stamp the passes for session 1. If you have time, lead straight into one or both of the following quick games.

◖◗2 Spot the difference
⊞ ◷◷ *(5–10 minutes)*

What you do
Invite adult helpers (briefed in advance) to parade in front of the children in the style of a fashion show. You could provide a suitable commentary to make it more fun. If appropriate, encourage the children to mime being press photographers and take imaginary photos. Tell the children to study each person carefully because they will return in a moment, but something about them will have changed.

After each parade, the adult helpers change something about themselves, such as not wearing glasses, a change of hairstyle, or adding a jacket. As the game progresses, make it more difficult with very subtle changes, such as removing an earring or wearing a watch on the opposite wrist. Ask the children to spot the difference. Repeat this several times – it's a good way to introduce the team to everyone.

◖◗3 Grab-a-gran
◷◷ *(5 minutes)*

What you do
Play tag with one person wearing an item associated with a granny (or grandad), such as a shawl tied around the shoulders or a walking stick. (Avoid using head gear, for hygienic reasons, or anything that can be pulled tight around the neck.) The granny or grandad wears the shawl until they catch someone. That person then becomes the granny or grandad and wears the shawl. Make sure the adult helpers join in with this activity too – it makes it more fun.

☺ *They just loved Grab-a-gran!* ☺
Paula, Kendal

Session 1

**Luke
4:38–40**

Aim **To discover the difference Jesus made in Peter's house. He can make a difference in the home of each child in Streetwise.**

Notes for you
Jesus changed Peter's mother-in-law's life in a dramatic way, demonstrating his power and authority over sickness, as well as his care and concern for individuals. As you introduce **Streetwise**, pray that the children will understand the impact that Jesus has on people and experience his saving love for themselves.

Checklist
- A 'Luke Street' sign, on display (page 19)
- A **Streetwise** pass (photocopied from page 20 onto thin card) and a pen for each child
- A copy of Luke's Gospel for each child, or a photocopy of the Bible verses on page 15 for each child (optional)
- Materials for your choice of activities for *Open the door*, *Step inside* and *Make yourself at home*

⊞ *When you see this logo, the activity is particularly appropriate for smaller groups.*

◷◷ *When you see this logo, the activity will also work well with older children.*

1

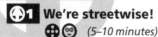

Step inside

1 We're streetwise!
⊞ ☺ *(5–10 minutes)*

Teach your group 'Streetwise', the **Streetwise** song, either using the DVD or the recording on *Light for Everyone* (track 14).

2 See the film
⊞ ☺ *(5 minutes)*

Explain that the first person in Luke Street wouldn't have been in the mood for visitors because she was very ill. Show 'The Sick House' from the **Streetwise** DVD.

> *They sat amazingly still and quiet for this – we had 24 children – and it led very nicely into the prayer bandage and sharing about friends and relatives who were ill.*
> *Sarah, Gloucester*

3 Read the book
⊞ ☺ *(3 minutes)*

What you need
- A copy of Luke's Gospel for each child, or a photocopy of the Bible verses on page 15 for each child (optional)

What you do
Tell the children that Luke Street is named after Luke, who was a writer. He wrote a book that was named after him, too. The story they have just watched is from the book of Luke.

It's a true story. It really happened, just over two thousand years ago. Luke wrote it down so that people all over the world could hear about Jesus and how he changed people's lives. This is what Luke wrote.

Read, or ask a confident reader to read **Luke 4:38–40**. If appropriate, encourage the children to find and follow the verses for themselves. Alternatively, ask at least two children to mime each verse. There are only three verses, and each has plenty of action!

4 Drama: At the surgery
⊞ *(5–10 minutes)*

What you need
- Two copies of the script
- A table and two chairs
- Two biblical style headdresses (optional)

What you do
The drama should be rehearsed in advance. If you are short of adult helpers, consider asking members of your church youth group to present the drama. The two actors sit facing each other across the table. That way, they can have the scripts in front of them on the table.

Alternatively, improvise the drama as a role play. Peter's mother-in-law visits her doctor to tell him the amazing thing that happened when she was very ill and Jesus visited her house.

■ SCENE 1
The doctor is seated at table. Mother-in-law enters.

Doctor: *(Shakes hands with mother-in-law.)* Good morning. Please sit down. I understand from your son-in-law, who made the appointment, that you need to register with me as your new doctor. Is that right?

Mother-in-law: That's right doctor. My daughter suggested I register with you. I'm not sure why I actually need to see you. I haven't had a day's illness in years. But now I am an old woman, I do as I'm told.

Doctor: It's usual to give people a quick check-up before they sign on. It also gives you a chance to meet me and see what you think.

Mother-in-law: *(Looking at him with a critical eye.)* Mm, you'll do.

Doctor: So you live with your daughter and her family. How are you coping with that? Any problems? More housework? Extra babysitting? I know sometimes these things aren't easy.

Mother-in-law: Well, I don't mind telling you, what gets me is the smell of fish! I don't know how my daughter stands it. I told her when she fell in love with that Peter, she'd smell of fish for the rest of her life.

Doctor: But with a son-in-law who's a fisherman, you'll be eating plenty of fish at home and that's very healthy and good for your bones.

Mother-in-law: I don't care if fish is healthy, it still smells! When Peter comes into the house it's like being hit in the face with a wet kipper.

Doctor: Hmm. Well, as far as your general health, you are as fit as a fiddle. Obviously at your age you need to keep as calm as possible. Don't let fishy things upset you. Lie down in the afternoons. That kind of thing.

Mother-in-law: All right doctor. Thank you. Goodbye. *(Mother-in-law exits.)*

■ SCENE 2
The doctor is seated at table. Mother-in-law enters. The doctor asks the following questions and the mother-in-law improvises short answers, emphasising the amazing thing that Jesus did.

1

Doctor: I heard about you being ill last week, what happened? What do you think it was? A bug? Something you ate? I hear that Jesus was around to help. What did he do – give you some tablets? Did you feel a bit wobbly afterwards and have to spend a few days in bed recovering?
Doctor: *(After the last question.)* I'm amazed! Oh, by the way, do you think you could come and cook me and my family a meal?!

Make yourself at home

Choose from the following activities, making sure you choose at least one of the Powerhouse activities:

01 **Streetwise cafe**
 *(5–10 minutes)*

What you need

- Part of your meeting area set up as a small cafe, with a few tables and chairs if possible (if you want to be really ambitious, you could have a sun umbrella in a stand, tablecloths, flowers on the tables and simple menus!)
- Refreshments for the children – remember to check for any food allergies children might have and avoid nuts

What you do

Ask the children for suggestions of what Peter's mother-in-law might have cooked for the children. Reassure them that you won't be dishing up lentil stew! Encourage the adult helpers to serve the refreshments to the children, taking 'orders' if appropriate. Remember that supportive church members are often happy to help with catering. Encourage them to vary the food for each session and be creative in what they provide. Remember that the **Streetwise** cafe is a good opportunity to chat with the children. If you do 'Cafe quiz', do it while the children are still sitting at the tables and chairs.

02 **Cafe quiz**
(5 minutes)

What you need

- Paper plates and serviettes, with the following numbered questions written on the paper plates, and the answers on the serviettes (*not* numbered)
- A 'Today's special' board (made from a large

sheet of paper) for the final question
- Pens for older children for the final question (optional)

■ NUMBERED QUESTIONS
(FOR THE PAPER PLATES)
1 What was Peter's other name?
2 Whose mother was Peter's mother-in-law – his or his wife's?
3 What was wrong with Peter's mother-in-law?
4 Who went to Peter's home when his mother-in-law was ill?
5 What did Jesus do?
6 Can doctors order a fever to go away?
7 Why did the local doctors have a holiday?

■ ANSWERS (FOR THE PAPER SERVIETTES)
1 Simon
2 Peter's wife's mother
3 She had a high fever
4 Jesus
5 He ordered the fever to go away
6 No
7 Because Jesus healed lots of people

What you do

Distribute the paper plates and serviettes amongst the children while they sit at the **Streetwise** cafe. If you have a small group, the children could have several plates and serviettes each. If you have a large group, make sure you don't miss anyone out – children could share if necessary. In turn, invite children with a numbered paper plate to read the question, or bring you their plate for you to read for them. The children with serviettes check to see if they think the answer they have on their serviette is the answer for that question.

When you have finished the quiz, explain that there is a final question that doesn't have an answer written down on a serviette. The final question is: **what does this story tell us about Jesus?** Older children could write their answer to the final question on the back of a plate or serviette. Younger children could talk about their answers with an adult helper. When you have discussed the children's answers, they could write them on the 'Today's special' board if appropriate.

03 **Down your street**
(10 minutes)

What you need

- Two signs – 'Peter's problem' and 'Your problem?'
- A Bible marked at **Luke 4:38–40** – one for each group

1

- Comfortable, informal seating such as bean bags or cushions (optional)

What you do

These questions could be presented to the whole group, or the children could discuss them in small groups with an adult helper, using a Bible.

Show the 'Your problem?' sign, then ask questions like these non-threatening, open questions. Adapt them according to the size of your group.

1 Have you got any grannies? What are they like? (Or ask a similar question leading to an explanation of 'mother-in-law'.)
2 Have you ever had any 'big' illnesses in your family? What happens in your home when someone is ill?
3 Can you remember the last time you had a high temperature? How did you feel?
4 How do you feel when people in your family are ill?
5 How do you feel when something is wrong, either in your family or for yourself, and you can't change it? (Be prepared to give an example.)

Show the 'Peter's problem' sign then ask the following questions. Encourage the children to look at **Luke 4:38–40** as they think about their answers.

1 What did Peter do about his problem?
2 Who solved Peter's problem?

Show the 'Your problem?' sign again and ask these questions.

1 What problems might you have?
2 Thinking about this story, what might we do if we have a problem?

■ THOUGHTS FOR LEADERS

The questions begin with ordinary life, questions to make conversation easy and to help everyone feel comfortable. Be prepared to talk about your own experiences and situations where God has and has not made people better. This is a potentially painful subject which will recur as you encounter other stories of healing in Luke. Children unfamiliar with Christian faith may find this a new or confusing idea. Pray for wisdom to talk openly about the fact that Jesus did and does heal and wants to make a difference, especially at times of hardship.

■ POSSIBLE CONFUSIONS

- If the version of the Bible you use has a name that is not the same as the one on the DVD, remember to explain the reason for this and that it is the same person.
- Many children will find it strange the way the

names of Jesus and God are used interchangeably. (Did God make the woman better? Did Jesus?) The questions presume a link between Jesus in the story, a concrete person they encountered in the Bible reading and watching the DVD, and the Jesus we know, who can make a difference to their lives now. This is a deliberate presumption but we need to be aware that it could be a confusing jump in thinking.

⑦4 Streetwise virtual reality
(15–30 minutes)

What you need

- Copies of the templates on page 21 to use as guides or to cut out
- Paper
- Paint
- Scissors, pencils and glue
- Large and small boxes (optional)

What you do

'**Streetwise** virtual reality' can be achieved, but without a computer! This could be an ongoing activity, with everyone working on the street over the eight sessions, perhaps doing one house per session. Create the different houses in Luke Street in miniature, or even have a go at constructing life-size replicas! If you have a small group and limited resources, take a 'small is beautiful' approach. Alternatively, each child could make individual houses with matchboxes, or small boxes from shoe shops. Or paint a mural or design a collage with the children, adding to it each session. If you're able to 'think big', try to involve parents – especially if they are builders or structural engineers! Get hold of large packing boxes such as those used for household appliances. The houses could be tall enough to enter with opening doors cut in the cardboard, but could be constructed as facades, similar to those on a film set. Each house front could be different even if you use the same type of boxes.

Divide the children into small groups to work on a house, or part of one. This will help them 'own' their house and also get to know each other better while they work together. If it is practical, each group could have their own house to use like a den. However, you may prefer to have just one house, and change it slightly each week for the specific story. If houses are impractical for your venue, create different doors instead. Make these from paper, which can be rolled up for storage at the end of each session.

⏱5 What do you think?
⊕ 😐 *(5 minutes)*

What you need
- The children's **Streetwise** passes
- Felt-tip pens or pencils

What you do

At the end of the session, encourage the children to think about what they remember most about today's programme and write or draw it in the space for The Sick House on the back of their **Streetwise** pass. This may be a game, the film or even a response to the teaching of this session. Help any children as necessary. The children will build up a reminder of what they learnt and experienced in the club over the eight sessions.

Powerhouse

Choose one or both of these prayer ideas. *(5–10 minutes)*

Today's special prayers ⊕

What you need
- The 'Today's special' board from the final question in 'Cafe quiz'

What you do

Introduce the time of prayer with the words, 'Thank you, God, because Jesus is…' then invite everyone in turn to read the responses to Jesus that they wrote on the board, as prayers of praise and thanks.

Bandage prayers 😐

What you need
- A long, white bandage, or several bandages if you divide the children into groups
- Felt-tip pens

What you do

Use the felt-tip pens to write on the bandage the names of people who are ill or sad or in any kind of need. As well as remembering family, friends and people close to home, encourage everyone to think about world needs, such as disaster areas, homeless people and countries where people are starving.

Display the bandage or bandages and either read the names aloud or invite everyone to pray silently for the people whose names are written on them.

☺ We always have a simple prayer time and the kids who want to – which is usually 80 per cent of them – come up and say their please or thank you bit. This tends to keep the discipline as well as keeping them involved. With more than forty kids, some of whom can't read or write, the only way we could do it was to get them to shout out the words to describe God and shout out the names of people who needed help, and a leader wrote it down and then prayed for them. It was noisier than normal and I don't think they felt so involved. We will need to work on this over the next few weeks. ☹

Dougie, Evesham

Session 2

Luke
5:17–26

Aim **To realise Jesus showed he had power to forgive sins and heal sick people. Jesus knows what we are like inside and can forgive us too.**

THE CROWDED HOUSE

Notes for you

When confronted with the paralysed man, Jesus demonstrated his divine authority to forgive sins, as well as his power to heal. He ministered to the man's spiritual as well as physical needs. Imagine the children in your group at the feet of Jesus. Pray for them by name and mention any specific needs.

When you see this logo, the activity is particularly appropriate for smaller groups.

When you see this logo, the activity will also work well with older children.

Open the door

As the children arrive, date stamp their Streetwise pass. Gather everyone together and welcome them to Streetwise. Remind the children of the adult helpers' names. Give out any notices at this point and mention any children who have had birthdays since your last session. Choose some or all of the activities below, according to the time you have.

1 Busy bodies
(5 minutes)

What you do

Ask the children to show everyone any weird and wonderful things they can do with their bodies, such as wiggle their ears or touch their nose with their tongue. Take it in turns and encourage all the children to do something – everyone can pull a strange face. Vote for the funniest and the most unusual party trick.

Invite everyone to lie on the floor and do a simple task, such as lifting his or her leg in the air. Then ask them to lift the other leg. This time, stop them before they do it and ask them to imagine that they are paralysed and can't move at all. How does that make them feel? Talk about it together.

2 Impossible?
(5 minutes)

What you need
- A sheet of A4 paper for each person
- Scissors

What you do

Give everyone a sheet of paper each. Ask them to make a hole in it and step through the hole without tearing the paper!

These diagrams show how it can be done:

1 Fold the paper in half.

2 Make four cuts from the centre fold up to 2 cm from the edge of the paper.

3 Turn the paper around and make three cuts in between the first cuts, from the edge of the paper to 2 cm from the fold.

4 Cut along the middle three folds, but don't cut the two end sections!

5 Open out the paper and step through the hole!

One boy managed to cut a very narrow edge of a piece of A4 paper and got his body through it! I really like this trick, but it needs to be well rehearsed before trying to show it to the children.
Sue, Yate

A number of children were going to take this home to test out on their parents/carers.
Wendy, Nottingham

2 Stretcher case
(10–15 minutes)

What you need
- Two pairs of track suit bottoms
- Two T-shirts or sweatshirts
- Two hats
- Two balloons
- Lots of newspaper
- Elastic bands or string and scissors
- Two sheets or blankets
- A skipping rope for the obstacle course (optional)

What you do

Divide the children into two groups and allocate

at least one adult helper to each group.

Give the groups at least five minutes to create a stuffed 'man' with the clothes and newspaper. The best way to do this is to scrunch up newspaper, stuff it into the clothes and secure the ends of arms and legs with string or elastic bands. Attach the balloon for the head.

When the time is up, admire the finished creations. Then give each group a sheet or towel and ask them to make a stretcher to carry their man.

Invite the groups to race each other with their 'man' on the stretcher (preferably with one person holding each corner) around an obstacle course. Keep the course very simple (such as under a table, around a chair and over a rope held off the ground by two adult helpers). Time the race, or do it as a relay. You could link this activity to the previous activity, 'Impossible?', and for a finale, the groups could push their stuffed man through the hole they create in the paper 'roof'.

Step inside

◔1 We're streetwise!
⊕ ☺ *(2 minutes)*

What you do
It's time for the next visit to Luke Street! Sing the **Streetwise** song together, reminding the children of the tune and words, if necessary.

◔2 See the film
⊕ ☺ *(5 minutes)*

Explain that this person in Luke Street had to rely on his friends to help him, because he couldn't walk. Show 'The Crowded House' from the **Streetwise** DVD.

◔3 Read the book
⊕ ☺ *(3 minutes)*

What you do
Ask the children to pretend that they are news reporters, trying to find out what happened in Luke Street. Read **Luke 5:17–26** to them in an excited way, as if you are giving them an eyewitness account.

For younger children, enlarge the Bible text and print it onto an acetate with a 5 cm-wide column to the left. As you read through the story, ask two children with a water-soluble pen

to draw a matchstick man on his mat – as he is carried up the stairs, as he is lowered through the roof and after he has been healed.

◔4 In the surgery
⊕ *(5–10 minutes)*

What you do
If you have team members who are good at drama, devise your own drama around the theme of the paralysed man. Alternatively, there is a script for you to develop at www.scriptureunion.org.uk/streetwise
Before The man is taken to the surgery for a check-up, establishing the usual routine of the paralysed man and the fact that he will not get better. Mention his friends.
After The amazing truth: he can walk! Telling the doctor and shared surprised gladness.

In discussion afterwards, explore some of these questions:
1 Have you got one best friend or do you have a group?
2 When have your friends done something so kind for you that you were surprised?
3 What do you think the man might have thought about what his friends did?
4 Do you find it hard to forgive people? Say why/why not, if you can.
5 Do you think, ever, that when you do something wrong God might mind? Do you think God cares whether we do right or wrong?
6 In what ways is Jesus different from ordinary people and in what ways is he the same?

■ THOUGHTS FOR LEADERS
You might want to move from questions about friendship to discussing forgiveness. Don't move on to the new start possible through Jesus' forgiveness unless they are ready for it. These issues will be revisited later in the stories. The crucifixion story allows plenty of discussion about this. Most children will have some awareness of wrongdoing. It might be enough to introduce the idea that God cares about this. Be careful about how you talk about 'sin'. It can be unfamiliar or have strange church-word associations.

Checklist
• A 'Luke Street' sign, on display (page 19)
• The children's **Streetwise** passes, ready to check and date stamp as they arrive and spare copies for any newcomers
• A copy of Luke's Gospel for each child, or a photocopy of the Bible verses on page 15 for each child (optional)
• Materials for your choice of activities for *Open the door, Step inside* and *Make yourself at home*

2

2

Make yourself at home

Choose from the following activities, making sure you do at least one of the Powerhouse activities:

Streetwise cafe
⊕ ⊕ *(5–10 minutes)*

What you do

Make, or get the children to make, ice-cream sodas by adding a scoop of ice cream to a fizzy drink. A straw and a slice of fruit make each drink a bit special.

⊕2 Bible brainstretcher
⊕ ⊕ *(5 minutes)*

What you need
- A photocopy of the Bible verses on page 15 for each child
- Coloured felt-tip pens (optional)

What you do

Make sure that there are plenty of people to help the younger children with this activity – either older children or adult helpers.

Ask the children to use felt-tip pens on their copy of the Bible verses in the following ways:
1 Draw a coloured line under the words that show *why* Jesus was able to heal people. (verse 17)
2 Use a different colour to draw a line under the words that show that lots of people wanted Jesus to help them. (verse 18)
3 Draw circles around the two things that Jesus did for the man. (verses 20 and 23)
4 Draw a zigzag line under the words that show that Jesus had healed the man. (verse 25)
5 Draw a wiggly line under the words that show what all the people did when they saw the man walking. (verse 26)

3 Luke's luggage
⊕ *(5–10 minutes)*

What you need
- A felt-tip pen
- A bag containing the following items:
- A small piece of material to represent a mat
- A line of four cut-out paper men
- A Lego roof tile or some pieces of straw
- The word 'sins' written on a piece of paper
- A picture of a happy person

What you do

Before the session, place the items in the bag. Invite the children to shut their eyes and pull an item out of the bag, one at a time. This is a good opportunity to involve shy or quiet children who wouldn't normally volunteer to do anything. Discuss each item, inviting the children to explain what part of the story of the paralysed man they think it represents.

For the 'sins' sheet of paper, explain that sin is the word the Bible uses for the things that we do, say and think that are wrong, and not what God wants. If appropriate, use the pen to write specific things on the paper that we do, and that the man might have done – things that the Bible says we should not do.

Ask the children what happened to the man's sins and at that point, tear up the piece of paper to demonstrate that Jesus forgave the man for those things.

Explain that Jesus wants to forgive us too. If we are really sorry for our sins – the things we have done wrong – and ask Jesus to forgive us, he will! Isn't that amazing?

⊕4 Pick up your mat!
⊕ *(10 minutes)*

What you need
- An A4 piece of paper for each person
- An assortment of different coloured paper strips, cut width-wise from A4 paper

What you do
1 Draw a border on an A4 sheet of paper.

2 Within the border, cut slits about 1 cm apart, either horizontally or vertically.

3 Thread the coloured strips through, alternating them to form a woven pattern.

For extra effect, laminate the mats to turn them into place mats. That way the children could use them at the **Streetwise** cafe or take them home. Take the opportunity to chat with the children while they are doing this activity.

☺*It took time to prepare this for the younger children.* ☺

Dougie, Evesham

⏱5 Streetwise virtual reality
⊕ *(15–30 minutes)*

What you need
- The materials you are using to create Luke Street (see page 32)

What you do
Continue working on your version of Luke Street. Remember this is a great time to get alongside the children and chat with them while you work.

⏱6 What do you think?
⊕ ☺ *(5 minutes)*

What you need
- The children's **Streetwise** passes
- Felt-tip pens or pencils

What you do
At the end of the session, encourage the children to think about what they remember most about today's programme and write or draw it in the space for The Crowded House on the back of their **Streetwise** pass. This may be a game, the film or their own response to the teaching of this session. Help any children as necessary. Can the children make any connection between the last session's story and this one?

Powerhouse

Choose one or both of these prayer ideas. *(5 minutes)*

Forgiven! ⊕ ☺

What you need
- A piece of paper and a pen or pencil for each person
- A rubbish bin

What you do
Remind everyone of the part of the story where Jesus tells the man his sins are forgiven. Invite anyone who wants to, to write or draw things they would like to ask God to forgive them for. Make sure there is no pressure on the children to do this and assure them that no one else will see what they have put. Invite everyone to fold the paper and ask God silently to forgive them for those things. Then encourage everyone to tear their paper up and throw the pieces in the bin, as a sign that he has forgiven them. Finish with a simple prayer of thanks for God's forgiveness.

> ☺ *Due to writing problems, we said they could draw a picture, or if the spelling wasn't right, God would still know what they meant!* ☺
> Dougie, Evesham

Thank you! ☺

What you do
Say this prayer a line at a time, pausing after each line. Invite the children to pray it silently after you if they want to:

Thank you, God, that you know all about me, just like Jesus knew all about the man who couldn't walk.
Thank you that you know me inside out.
Thank you that you want to help me on the inside as well as the outside.
Thank you for forgiving me when I am sorry for the wrong things I have done.
Amen.

> ☺ *One girl's grandma had died this week. So we prayed for the family.* ☺
> Sarah, Gloucester

Session 3

Luke
7:36–40,44–50

Aim To hear of a woman who was grateful Jesus had forgiven her and who showed how much she loved him. We can show Jesus how grateful we are that he has forgiven us.

Notes for you

While Jesus was eating at the home of a Pharisee, a woman with a reputation for being a sinner visited the house, intending to anoint Jesus with expensive perfume. However, she was overcome with remorse and her tears of repentance landed on Jesus' feet as she expressed her love and gratitude for his forgiveness. Rather than condemning her, Jesus rebuked his host who had not given him the treatment due to a guest and reassured the woman that all her sins were forgiven. Pray that the children will understand how much Jesus loves them and wants to forgive them.

 When you see this logo, the activity is particularly appropriate for smaller groups.

 When you see this logo, the activity will also work well with older children.

THE RICH HOUSE

Open the door

As the children arrive, date stamp their Streetwise pass. Gather everyone together and welcome them to Streetwise. If there are newcomers, introduce them to everyone. Give out any notices at this point and mention any children who have had birthdays since your last session. Choose some or all of the activities below, according to the time you have.

◀▶1 Footsteps
(5–10 minutes)

What you need

- Large footprint shapes cut out of newspaper – enough for one per child and two or three extra
- A CD/cassette player and music

What you do

Place the footprint shapes on the floor and spread them out to cover the available space. Play this game like Musical Chairs. Play the music. When it stops, each person has to stand on a footprint shape. Gradually remove the footprint shapes. If a child cannot find a footprint to stand on, they are out.

◀▶2 Perfume factory
 (10 minutes)

What you need

- A clear plastic bottle or cup – enough for one per team
- An ice-cream tub full of water – enough for one per team
- A plastic spoon – enough for one for each person

What you do

This game is best played outside. Divide everyone (children and adult helpers) into teams of five or six people. Give each person a plastic spoon. Place an ice-cream tub full of water next

to each team and a cup or bottle about two or three metres away from them.

Explain that everyone is working in a perfume factory. Their task is to fill a container of perfume (the cup or bottle) from the vat of perfume (the ice-cream tub of water) that each team has, but they have to use spoons to do it! Give the teams a time limit. They can either run in turn to the bottle or container with a spoonful of water, or transfer the water from spoon to spoon in a human chain. When the time is up, compare the cups or bottles to see which team has filled their container with the most perfume.

You may only want to do this in the summer!

◀▶3 Get a whiff of this!
 (5–10 minutes)

What you need

- A variety of smells (most of which can be kept in their original containers), such as tea, coffee, lemon juice, peanut butter, vinegar, mustard, mint sweets, perfumed soap, pot-pourri, banana, blackcurrant juice, disinfectant, soap powder, curry powder and yeast extract (Marmite or Vegemite)
- Blindfolds

What you do

Blindfold the children and ask them to identify a smell. Make sure everyone has a turn. If you have a large group, two or three children could try to guess the same smell. With a smaller group, the children could have two smells to identify. At the end, the children could vote for the worst smell and the best smell.

> ❺ *This was popular and kept the groups busy for quite a while!* ❺
> *Sue, Yate*

Step inside

⏱1 We're streetwise!
⊕ ☺ *(2 minutes)*

What you do
Sing the **Streetwise** song, as it's time for another trip down Luke Street.

⏱2 See the film
⊕ ☺ *(5 minutes)*

What you need
• A perfume or eau de cologne atomiser

What you do
Spray some perfume in the air, then explain to the children that it would be easy to find the house that Jesus visited in Luke Street this time – you could smell it! Show 'The Rich House' from the **Streetwise** DVD.

⑤ They remembered last week's story and the forgiveness of sins, and that carried through to this week's story. ⑤
Sarah, Gloucester

⏱3 Read the book
⊕ ☺ *(3 minutes)*

What you do
Choose three confident readers to read **Luke 7:36–40,44–50** (omitting verses 41–43). One person reads the words Jesus said, another takes the part of Simon and the third person reads everything else as a narrator. This should be rehearsed in advance.

Explain that in Jesus' time, roads were very dusty. When people arrived at someone's house for dinner, a servant would have washed the dust from the roads off their feet. People would greet each other with a kiss rather than shaking hands and it was a custom that visitors would have some oil poured over their head. It sounds strange to us, but it was what they did!

If appropriate for your group, invite everyone to take their shoes off and sit in the way that Jesus would have sat to eat the meal at Simon's house: lying on their left side, propped up on their left elbow. They should stay like this to listen to the Bible verses that tell them what happened during the meal.

⑤ We have printed out the title and theme of each session, so at the story time, we do a quick recap and build up the picture for the children. This seems to make a link between all the stories and gives the children a better picture of what we are exploring together. ⑤
Dougie, Evesham

⏱4 Drama: In the surgery
⊕ ☺ *(5–10 minutes)*

What you do
If you have team members who are good at drama, devise your own drama around the theme of the visit to Simon's house. Alternatively, there is a script for you to develop at www.scriptureunion.org.uk/streetwise
Before A servant from Simon's house, who is not well, comes to the doctor and while talking to him mentions that Jesus has been invited to a meal.
After The servant returns and tells the doctor about what happened during the meal.
Follow the drama with 'Quiet, quality questions for quickwits' (on page 40).

■ THOUGHTS FOR LEADERS
Some children, especially the older ones, may have questions about the woman's sinful life. They may find it surprising that Jesus mixed with people they might think of as 'unchurchy'. Basically this woman had lots of relationships with men which were not good for her and made other people look down on her. But Jesus did not look down on her, far from it.

Checklist
• A 'Luke Street' sign, on display (page 19)
• The children's **Streetwise** passes, ready to check and date stamp as they arrive and spare copies for any newcomers
• A copy of Luke's Gospel for each child, or a photocopy of the Bible verses on page 16 for each child (optional)
• Materials for your choice of activities for *Open the door, Step inside* and *Make yourself at home*

3

3

Make yourself at home

Choose from the following activities, making sure you include at least one of the Powerhouse activities:

Streetwise cafe
(5–10 minutes)

What you do

Serve the refreshments to the children as they recline in the way that Jesus and his friends would have done to eat a special meal – lying on their left side, propped up on their left elbow and using their right hand to eat. If you have a low coffee table, arrange the food on that and invite the children to recline around it. If possible, provide some cushions. Alternatively, everyone could sit cross-legged on the floor. Serve grape juice with biblical style food such as fresh and dried fruit, cheese, bread and cakes, but avoid nuts because of potential allergies.

Quiet, quality questions for quickwits
(10 minutes)

What you need

- The questions below, photocopied from page 22, cut into strips and placed in a hat or bag
- Each child's copy of the Bible verses, or a Bible for each group

What you do

Divide the children into small groups, each with at least one adult helper. If you have a small number of children, keep everyone together. Choose someone to pick a quiet, quality question for quickwits from the hat or bag. Read the question to everyone and give the groups a few minutes to discuss it. There is a mixture of question styles to encourage discussion and help the group members to apply the Bible to their lives. If you find that no one is responding to a particular question, choose another one – groups can move on at their own pace by selecting new questions at any time, reading it to their group and then replacing it in the hat or bag for another group.

1 Does anybody you know wear perfume? Do you like the smell?

2 Are you afraid of getting into trouble when you do something wrong?

3 When was the last time you were in trouble? What happened?

4 Do you ever cry when you have done something wrong? Why do you think you cry?

5 Have you ever owned up to something you have done, even when you had not been found out? Could you say why?

6 Sometimes at school or in families, some people are thought of as 'good' or 'bad'. Which would you want people to think of you?

7 Does it sometimes feel as if grown-ups want you to be good and other children think it's more exciting to be bad? What do you think?

8 What sort of things would you find difficult to forgive? (Check out Luke 6:37.)

9 How can we show Jesus we love him if we can't see him?

10 The woman's tears showed she was sorry. Check out 1 John 1:8,9. Do you think you can be forgiven if you *aren't* sorry?

Smelly sachets
(10 minutes)

What you need

- Squares of material or multi-packs of hankies (available from discount stores)
- Pot-pourri or lavender – enough for each child to have about two teaspoonfuls
- An elastic band and a piece of ribbon for each child

What you do

This is a quick, simple activity to remind the children about the woman who poured perfume on Jesus' feet. Boys might not be very keen to do this – but they could make one as a present for their mum or grandma.

The children should spread their hanky flat on a table and put the pot-pourri or lavender in the middle. They then gather the corners up and secure with the elastic band before tying the ribbon on.

As the children made their smelly sachets, some of them realised how everything linked together and what the woman had done.
Tricia, Swadlincote

ⓜ4 Streetwise virtual reality
 (15–30 minutes)

What you need
- The materials you are using to create Luke Street (see page 32)

What you do
Continue to create Luke Street. Use this activity as an opportunity to chat with the children you are working with.

ⓜ5 What do you think?
 (5 minutes)

What you need
- The children's **Streetwise** passes
- Felt-tip pens or pencils

What you do
At the end of the session, encourage the children to think about what they remember most about today's programme and write or draw it in the space for The Rich House on the back of their **Streetwise** pass. Was this a different thing from the last session? Help any children as necessary.

Powerhouse

Include one or both of these prayer activities in your programme.
(5 minutes)

Prayers on a plate

What you need
- A paper plate and a felt-tip pen for each person

What you do
If you do this activity before **Streetwise** cafe, use the paper plates for the cafe activity.

Give everyone a paper plate and a felt-tip pen and encourage them to find a space to do this activity. Explain that they should use the underside of their plate to write or draw on, so that no one else can see what they have put.

This is an opportunity for everyone to tell God anything they want to, especially if there are things that they are sorry for, things they want to thank him for (like the woman in the story) or things they want to ask him about. Stress that they can draw or write what they want to say – handwriting and spelling don't matter at all. When they have finished, give everyone a few minutes to pray quietly about what they have written or drawn. Suggest they keep their plate to use at the **Streetwise** cafe.

Pipe cleaner praise

What you need
- A chenille wire (pipe cleaner) for each child
- Background music and CD/cassette player

What you do
Give each child a chenille wire and ask them to shape it simply into something that is important to them, that they would like to give to Jesus. It could be a favourite toy or pet, or could be something they are good at, eg a computer, a pair of legs for sport or dance, a football. Play background music as they think. You may wish to talk about it or simply tell Jesus how much you love him and want to give him what is important to you. You may need to explain that we do not literally give things for him to take away, but it is more a case of sharing the ownership with him.

Luke
8:40–42,49–56

Aim **To realise that Jesus showed he had power to bring Jairus' daughter back to life. Nothing is impossible for Jesus – then and now.**

Notes for you

As well as healing people and forgiving their sins, Jesus demonstrated his complete power over death when he raised Jairus' daughter to life. Pray that the children will understand that, as God's Son, Jesus has power over everything.

 When you see this logo, the activity is particularly appropriate for smaller groups.

 When you see this logo, the activity will also work well with older children.

THE LEADER'S HOUSE

Open the door

As the children arrive, date stamp their Streetwise pass. Gather everyone together and welcome them to Streetwise. If there are newcomers, introduce them to everyone. Give out any notices at this point and mention any children who have had birthdays since your last session. Choose some or all of the activities below, according to the time you have.

◁)1 Sleepy?
☺ *(5 minutes)*

What you do

Ask the children to settle themselves into a comfortable position on the floor. They have to keep completely still. One or two adult helpers circulate, trying to make them laugh, but without touching them. Anyone spotted moving is out of the game. Whoever is left at the end of the time limit is a winner.

◁)2 Search party
⊕ *(5–10 minutes)*

What you do

Divide the children into groups. Ask which group can be first to find and bring you one of the following items:

A shoelace, a hair, a sock, a pencil, something red, a watch, a Bible, something heavy, a piece of paper, two left feet, a size 2 shoe, a 10-pence piece, someone whose name begins with S, a brother and sister, something made of cotton.

◁)3 Buzzing birthdays
☺ *(5 minutes)*

What you do

Line everyone up in age or birthday order. Help them do it the first time. They can do it themselves the second time. Make it a timed challenge.

Step inside

◔1 Be streetwise!
⊕ ☺ *(2 minutes)*

What you do

Sing the **Streetwise** song!

◔2 See the film
⊕ ☺ *(5 minutes)*

What you do

Explain that Jairus searched for Jesus to ask him to visit his house in Luke Street, before it was too late. Too late for what? Watch 'The Leader's House' from the **Streetwise** DVD to find out.

◔3 Read the book
⊕ ☺ *(3 minutes)*

What you do

Ask an adult helper who is a confident, dramatic reader to introduce themselves to everyone as one of the servants from Jairus' house. They should tell the children that Jesus did the most amazing thing and read **Luke 8:40–56**. Omit verses 43–48 if you feel the reading is too long, or is inappropriate for the group.

❻ We had 23 children present, the most so far. Some were there for the first time, so it was all new to them. The story of Jairus was acted by volunteer children. ❻

Sue, Yate

4 Drama: In the surgery
(5–10 minutes)

What you do
If you have team members who are dramatically inclined, prepare a drama in advance which explores what happened to Jairus' daughter. Alternatively, there is a script for you to develop at www.scriptureunion.org.uk/streetwise
Before Jairus' servant visits the doctor seeking some help for an earlier problem.
After The servant returns to tell the doctor what has happened.

Make yourself at home

Choose from the following activities, making sure you choose at least one of the Powerhouse activities:

1 Streetwise cafe
(5–10 minutes)

Jairus would have been so happy when Jesus raised his daughter back to life. No doubt there would have been a celebration party for all the friends and neighbours! Organise a special **Streetwise** party at the **Streetwise** cafe.

What you need
- Balloons
- Coloured crêpe paper
- Sticky tape and string
- Scissors and staplers to share
- CD player and CDs for background music
- Party food such as crisps, cakes and chocolate biscuits

What you do
Give everyone a few minutes to decorate the cafe ready for the celebration party. Allocate small groups of children to different tasks, such as blowing up balloons, making streamers, decorating tables or even making simple party hats for everyone. Serve party food to the children and play background music.

The girls particularly liked the party!
Tricia, Swadlincote

2 Powerworks
(5 minutes)

What you do
Set the children five tasks that test their strength or endurance, eg hopping on one leg for 30 seconds, doing ten sit ups, a tug of war, carrying three yogurt pots piled on top of each other, running on the spot.

Afterwards, talk about how Jesus' power was different from this.

3 Luke's luggage
(5–10 minutes)

What you need
- A bag containing the following items:
- A family photograph to represent Jairus' family
- A pack of 12 birthday cake candles to indicate the girl's age
- A bottle of medicine
- A clock to indicate a sense of urgency
- Some party poppers to represent the surprise and rejoicing when the girl was raised to life – no one was expecting that!

What you do
Before the session, place the items in the bag. Invite children to shut their eyes and pull an item out of the bag, one at a time. This is a good opportunity to involve children who don't often get chosen to do things. Discuss each item, inviting the children to explain which part of the story it represents. Emphasise that nothing is impossible for Jesus, even bringing someone back to life.

Most children found this interesting and came up with some perceptive ideas about what each item might mean in the context of the story.
Sue, Yate

Checklist
- A 'Luke Street' sign, on display (page 19)
- The children's **Streetwise** passes, ready to check and date stamp as they arrive, plus spare copies for newcomers
- A copy of Luke's Gospel, or a photocopy of the Bible verses on page 16 for each child (optional)
- Materials for your choice of activities for *Open the door, Step inside* and *Make yourself at home*

4

⏱4 Down your street
⊕ ☺ *(10–15 minutes)*

What you need
• A photocopy of the questions below for each small group (optional)

What you do
Interview a suitable Christian adult using the questions below. It could be someone you know who has had to cope with illness or bereavement, who could share with the children what happened, how God answered their prayers and how they trusted him in difficult circumstances.

When the interview has finished, invite the children to ask questions. If appropriate, divide the children into small groups with an adult helper and go through some of the same questions.

1 Have you, or anyone you know, ever been really poorly?
2 Who helped you, and how?
3 Sometimes God changes situations, but not always. Why do you think that is?
4 Why do people have to die?
5 If you were Jairus' daughter, what would you have thought when you woke up?
6 How do you think Jairus felt about Jesus?
7 When Jesus did not come at once, Jairus might have thought he did not really understand or care. Have you ever felt like that when things don't happen the way you want? Can you tell us about it?

■ THOUGHTS FOR LEADERS
It's possible that children will be in situations of bereavement or sickness where there does not seem much hope of recovery. Be ready for questions about what happens when we die or why not everyone is made better. Children who are already part of a church community may have just as many odd ideas about heaven and dying as those who are unconnected with church. Be ready also with stories of Jesus at work in people's lives now, so the link is made between Jesus at work in the story and Jesus at work NOW.

⏱5 Just to say…
⊕ ☺ *(10–15 minutes)*

What you need
• Pieces of A4 card, folded in half
• A5 envelopes
• Coloured felt-tip pens
• Collage materials, scissors and glue (optional)

What you do
There may be people at your church or known to you who are ill and who would appreciate a card. As well as making cards, encourage the children to pray for people they know who are ill. Encourage the children to think carefully about the message on the card. Rather than 'Get well soon', they may want to say 'Thinking of you', or 'Praying for you'.

Alternatively, if you have time, you could ice some biscuits for someone who's ill.

❻ *The children thought most carefully about who their card was for.* ❾
Becky, Bedford

⏱6 Streetwise virtual reality
⊕ ☺ *(15–30 minutes)*

What you need
• The materials you are using to create Luke Street (see page 32)

What you do
Continue to create Luke Street.

◎7 What do you think?
◈ ☺ *(5 minutes)*

What you need
- The children's **Streetwise** passes
- Felt-tip pens or pencils

What you do
At the end of the session, encourage the children to think about what they remember most about today's programme and write or draw it in the space for The Leader's House on the back of their **Streetwise** pass. If the children are putting the same thing each week, encourage them to think of something else to remember. Help any children as necessary. What impressions do you get about what the children are getting out of the club? You might find it useful to use any comments the children make to help you with evaluating how the club is going – what activities have the children enjoyed the most? Which ways of exploring the Bible story have the children responded to the most? Use these thoughts to help you fill in the evaluation sheet (see page 25) and to inform your planning of the next sessions.

Powerhouse

Choose one or both of these prayer ideas. *(5–10 minutes)*

A private chat ☺

What you do
Invite everyone to find a space and lie on the floor. Encourage everyone to think about the girl that Jesus brought back to life. Start the prayer time by saying, 'Thank you, God, that nothing is impossible for you. Thank you that Jesus brought the little girl back to life. Thank you too for…'
(Pause for the children to pray silently or aloud as they wish.)

If appropriate, suggest that the group might also like to use the opportunity to pray silently for people they know who are not well.

After a few moments, ask everyone to sit up as a reminder of what happened in the story.

All shout together, 'Jesus is amazing and powerful!'

Postbox prayers ◈ ☺

What you need
- A piece of paper and an envelope for each person
- A pen for each person
- A box with a slot cut out, to represent a postbox

What you do
Give each person a piece of paper, an envelope and a pen. Invite them to write a prayer letter. It can be about anything they like and it will be private – spelling and handwriting don't matter! They may like to say sorry for things they have thought, said or done, or they could thank God that nothing is impossible for him. They could also ask him for, or about, anything. When they have finished, they can put the paper in the envelope, seal it and post it in the box.

(You will need to destroy the letters after the session.)

**Luke
10:38–42**

Aim **To discover that doing what Jesus wants is the best – serving him, but even more, spending time with him. How can we spend time with Jesus?**

THE GUEST HOUSE

Notes for you

Distracted by the busyness of everyday life and domestic duty, Martha became cross and resentful. Rebuking her gently, Jesus insisted that the most important thing was to be with him, listening to what he had to say. Pray that the **Streetwise** sessions will help the children to meet with Jesus and understand how important it is to live his way. Pray especially for any that are behaving in a way that is not helpful to the rest of the group and ask for God's patience and love as you deal with them.

When you see this logo, the activity is particularly appropriate for smaller groups.

When you see this logo, the activity will also work well with older children.

Open the door

As the children arrive, date stamp their Streetwise pass. Gather everyone together and welcome them to Streetwise. If there are newcomers, introduce them to everyone. Give out any notices at this point and mention any children who have had birthdays since your last session. Choose some or all of the activities below, according to the time you have.

1 Spring cleaning
(5–10 minutes)

What you need
- A duster and a dust pan and brush for each team
- A chair for each team, placed at the opposite end of the room

What you do
Divide everyone into teams of six to eight people. Ask each team to line up one behind the other, ready for a relay race. Give the first person in each team a duster and a dust pan and brush.

On the word 'Go!' the first person in each team runs around the chair, back to his or her team and joins the end of the line. When each person runs, they must brush the floor and flick the duster as they go. The next person does the same, and so on. The winning team is the first to finish.

2 Martha's kitchen
(5–10 minutes)

What you need
- A selection of at least 12 items that Martha might have had in her kitchen, such as a bucket, a mop, a broom, a duster, a jug, a bowl, a wooden spoon, some fruit, flour, salt, pepper, milk, eggs and cheese
- A tablecloth
- A pencil and paper for each small group

What you do
This is played in the same way as the game known as Kim's game. Divide the children into small groups, each with an adult helper, or ask them to get into twos or threes (but make sure no one gets left out). Display the items, one at a time, naming each one. Then cover them with the cloth and ask the groups to write down as many of the items that they can remember – the adult helper could write the list. The group that remembers most of the items, wins. Second time around, ask everyone to close their eyes while you remove an item. See which group can identify the missing item first. Do this several times.

3 Chaos in the kitchen!
(5–10 minutes)

What you need
- Two eggs, either hard-boiled or raw – the choice is up to you (if you choose raw eggs you will need to provide mopping-up facilities and some spare eggs!)

What you do
Divide everyone into two equal teams. Ask the teams to line up one behind the other, ready for a relay race. Give the first person in each team an egg. The teams pass their egg backwards down the line, over their heads and under their legs alternately. When the person at the back of the line receives the egg, they should run to the front and start again. The winning team is the first to finish, with the first person back at the front of the line.

❝ *We used a wooden spoon – not eggs!* ❞
Sarah, Gloucester

5

Step inside

⌖1 We're streetwise!
⊕ ☹ *(2 minutes)*

What you do

Sing the **Streetwise** song!

⌖2 See the film
⊕ ☹ *(5 minutes)*

What you do

Ask the children if they ever have visitors for a meal or to stay the night. What's it like in their house when guests arrive? For some families, this may be an unusual event. This is what happened when some people in Luke Street had a special visitor. Show 'The Guest House' from the **Streetwise** DVD.

⌖3 Read the book
⊕ ☺ *(3 minutes)*

What you do

Read **Luke 10:38–42**. Before the session, draw five blank faces on an acetate and ask the children to fill in the expressions – three for Martha, one for Mary and one for Jesus as you read the verses together.

⌖4 Drama: At the surgery
⊕ ☹ *(5–10 minutes)*

What you do

If you have team members who are dramatically inclined, prepare a drama in advance which explores what happened to Jairus' daughter. Alternatively, there is a script for you to develop at www.scriptureunion.org.uk/streetwise
Before Martha goes to the doctor with domestic ailments and injuries.
After Martha returns to tell him what has happened and what a difference it has made. Follow this up with 'Buzz!'.

Make yourself at home

Choose from the following activities, making sure you include at least one of the Powerhouse activities:

⊘1 Streetwise cafe
⊕ ☹ *(5–10 minutes)*

What you do

To link in with this session's domestic theme, if you have the facilities, consider asking a church member to cook pancakes for the children. Alternatively, if you have a small group, help them cook their own. If this is not possible, serve home-made cakes (provided by willing church members). Otherwise, doughnuts or flapjacks are usually very popular!

> ❝ *Four older girls came to help us with the cooking. We made bread with chocolate and dried fruit – it was a winner!* ❞
>
> *Dougie, Evesham*

⊘2 Buzz!
⊕ ☺ *(10–15 minutes)*

What you need

- A photocopy of the questions below for each buzz group leader:
1 What jobs do you help with at home? Do you ever have arguments at home about helping and who does most? If that happens, why do you think it does?
2 What do you like to eat? What is your favourite meal?
3 Why did Martha get cross with Mary?
4 Do you think Martha was wrong to be busy preparing things for the meal?
5 Are there some people who we need to listen to? Who, and why?
6 Who does most of the cooking and cleaning at home? Does it make them stressed?
7 Do you know anyone you enjoy listening to? Could you say why?
8 Do you ever talk to God? Have you ever felt he was talking to you? Can you explain?
9 In what ways can people listen to God now? What sort of things does he say?
10 What do you think we can learn from the story about Martha and Mary?

Checklist

- A 'Luke Street' sign, on display (page 19)
- The children's **Streetwise** passes, ready to check and date stamp as they arrive, plus spare copies for newcomers
- A copy of Luke's Gospel, or a photocopy of the Bible verses on page 16 for each child (optional)
- Materials for your choice of activities for *Open the door*, *Step inside* and *Make yourself at home*

5

What you do
Divide the children into small buzz groups, with at least one adult helper to lead each group. They should have a copy of the questions and ask different children to choose a number between one and ten. The groups then discuss that particular question. Each group can move at its own pace.

■ THOUGHTS FOR LEADERS
You will need to brief the adult helpers who are going to lead the buzz groups.

• They should be prepared to talk about how they feel God has spoken to them and to others. Talk about the variety of ways in which it might happen and talk about reading the Bible as a time to be with God and listen to him.
• Talk about *Snapshots* notes, that are available to help them (for details see page 12). If appropriate, give *Snapshots* notes to the children.
• Be sure to find out if they have a Bible at home, and arrange to lend them one if not.
• Remember to ask them regularly how they are getting on with reading the Bible for themselves.
• Perhaps you could organise a five-minute slot before, after or during each session to go through the day's verses with any children who would benefit from that sort of help and encouragement – probably most of them!

⑤*I said it was good to remember Jesus is always ready to listen to us and talk to us. I made it personal to me. One boy said, 'I never hear God.' I said I did, then the children who have started coming to church since joining the club said that they hear God speaking too.*⑨
Sue, Yate

⑰3 Action replay
⊕ *(10–15 minutes)*

What you do
Divide the children into small groups of at least three, but no more than seven.
    Give each group a copy of **Luke 10:38–42**. Allow ten minutes for each group to create a short play with four scenes as follows:
Scene 1: At the home of Martha and Mary, getting ready for visitors
Scene 2: Jesus and his disciples arrive at the house and are welcomed
Scene 3: Martha goes back into the kitchen on her own and gets cross

Scene 4: Martha goes to Jesus, who gently tells her that Mary has chosen the best thing
    Be available to offer help if it is needed. After ten minutes, each group shows their play to everyone else.

⑰4 Make a meal of it!
⊕ *(10 minutes, excluding preparation and cooking)*

What you need
• 1 ½ cups hot water
• 1 cup salt
• 4 cups plain flour

What you do
Before the session, make up the dough. Add the water to the salt and then gradually add the flour, until you have a soft dough. Use the dough to create food shapes for a meal, which should be baked for two hours, 150 C/300 F/Gas mark 2, and painted in the next session. Do this activity if you haven't already done any cooking this session.

⑰5 Streetwise virtual reality
⊕ *(15–30 minutes)*

What you need
• The materials you are using to create Luke Street (see page 32)

What you do
Continue to create Luke Street. Be encouraging when you talk to the children about what they have made. Remember, too, to praise them on working well together.

⊙6 What do you think?
⊞ ☺ (5 minutes)

What you need
- The children's **Streetwise** passes
- Felt-tip pens or pencils

What you do
At the end of the session, encourage the children to think about what they remember most about today's programme and write or draw it in the space for The Guest House on the back of their **Streetwise** pass. Help any children as necessary. Chat with the children about **Streetwise** so far, as they fill in their passes.

☾ *It has been a growing realisation for me that doing all the work in the world is not an alternative to actually spending time with God. It is quite a grown-up concept to grasp, but the whole session worked well and I hope the children came away with some understanding of it. I know it helped me!* ☾

Sarah, Gloucester

Powerhouse

Choose one or both of these prayer ideas. *(5 minutes)*

Help! ⊞ ☺

What you need
- A Bible, marked at the following verses: Matthew 11:28; Matthew 28:20b; Luke 11:28; Luke 12:7; John 14:27

What you do
Invite the children to sit quietly in a space on the floor. Ask them to think about times when they feel like Martha did. Perhaps they get worried or cross, like she was, or maybe there are things that make them unhappy or scared. Ask them what they could do when they feel like that. Remind them that they can talk to God at any time, and they can listen to him too,

like Mary did. Explain that they can listen now to some things Jesus said. Ask different adult helpers to read some or all of the Bible verses, pausing between each one. When all the verses have been read aloud, encourage the children to pray silently about the things they thought of earlier and ask God to help them.

tsp ⊞ ☺

What you need
- A plastic teaspoon for each person (available in multi-packs from supermarkets)

What you do
Ask if anyone knows what the letters t s p stand for and where you would find them ('tsp' is an abbreviation for

teaspoon – often found in a recipe book). Explain that the letters tsp can remind us of three things we can say when we pray:
 'Thank you'
 'Sorry'
 'Please'
 We are very good at asking for things, but we don't always remember to say 'thank you' and 'sorry'. Encourage everyone to hold their teaspoon and pray, making sure they say 'thank you', 'sorry' *and* 'please'.

Luke
19:1–10

Aim **To hear how Jesus was prepared to befriend Zacchaeus. He wants everyone to be his friend, however unpopular they may be.**

THE CHEAT'S HOUSE

Notes for you

Zacchaeus wanted to see Jesus from his vantage point in the tree, but never expected Jesus to be interested in *him* – he was a cheat! But, of course, Jesus had come to save people like Zacchaeus, who needed to be changed. Pray that the children will understand that Jesus wants them to be his friends, and offers them the same love, forgiveness and acceptance that he gave to Zacchaeus.

When you see this logo, the activity is particularly appropriate for smaller groups.

When you see this logo, the activity will also work well with older children.

Open the door

As the children arrive, date stamp their Streetwise pass. Gather everyone together and welcome them to Streetwise. If there are newcomers, introduce them to everyone. Give out any notices at this point and mention any children who have had birthdays since your last session. Choose some or all of the activities below, according to the time you have.

1 Fortunately, unfortunately
(5–10 minutes)

What you do

This game will be followed up in *Make yourself at home*, relating specifically to this session's Bible verses.

Ask everyone to sit in a circle. Start with two sentences along the following lines: '*Fortunately*, my alarm clock went off this morning.' '*Unfortunately*, it's raining today.' Invite the next person in the circle to add a sentence that starts with the word 'Fortunately', such as, '*Fortunately*, I have an umbrella with me.' The next person in the circle could say, '*Unfortunately*, my umbrella is broken.' Continue the game for as long as possible saying, 'Fortunately, unfortunately' alternately around the circle.

2 Coin collectors
(5–10 minutes)

What you need
• A supply of foil-covered chocolate coins

What you do

Organise this like an Easter egg hunt and hide the coins around the room before the children arrive. If your supplies are limited, the children could be told to sit down as soon as they have found a certain number of coins. Alternatively, the coins could be hidden one at a time (like the game Hunt the Thimble), with 'cold', 'warm' or 'hot' as helpful hints. Once the coin is found, the finder can eat the coin and then hide the next one while the next 'finder' faces in the opposite direction and closes their eyes.

3 Hush-hush cash
(5 minutes)

What you need
• A bowl of coins
• A blindfold

What you do

Ask everyone to sit in a circle, facing inwards. Blindfold a volunteer who then sits in the middle of the circle with the bowl of coins on the floor next to them. Point at someone sitting in the circle. They have to sneak up and try to retrieve a coin without being intercepted. The blindfolded volunteer has to point at suspicious sounds. If caught by a pointing finger, the person trying to retrieve a coin is out. The game could be played in reverse, with people in the circle trying to return the money to the bowl.

4 Tax office, house or tree?
(5–10 minutes)

What you need
• A blindfold

What you do

Blindfold a volunteer and ask him or her to stand in a corner, facing away from everyone. Designate three different areas of the room (preferably corners) as a tax office, a house and a tree. Invite everyone to move around the room until the blindfolded volunteer calls out 'Tax office!' or 'House!' or 'Tree!' The last person to reach the named area is out.

Repeat this as many times as necessary, changing the blindfolded volunteer from time to time.

Step inside

⏱1 Be streetwise!
(2 minutes)

What you do
Sing the **Streetwise** song!

⏱2 See the film
(5 minutes)

What you do
No one thought Jesus would visit *this* person's house in Luke Street, but were they right? Watch 'The Cheat's House' from the **Streetwise** DVD.

Some children were worried by the size of Zacchaeus' nose and that people unkindly called him 'Titch'.
Sarah, Gloucester

⏱3 Read the book
(3 minutes)

What you do
Ask two adult helpers to take the part of Jesus and Zacchaeus, and mime as you read **Luke 19:1–10**. At the point where Zacchaeus climbs a tree, the person taking his part could stand on a chair. You will need to practise this before the session. If you have copies available, encourage everyone to follow the verses for themselves.

⏱4 Drama: At the surgery
(5–10 minutes)

What you do
If you have team members who are dramatically inclined, prepare a drama in advance which explores what happened to Zacchaeus. Alternatively, there is a script for you to develop at www.scriptureunion.org.uk/streetwise
Before Zacchaeus visits the doctor to ask about his height (and other problems).
After Zacchaeus returns to talk about how he feels about himself now.

This story is beautifully told in the book *Jesus and the Cheat* (SU) by Diane Walker, from the *Hands up* series. This book is available in 'big book' format, for details, see page 62.

Make yourself at home

Choose from the following activities, making sure you choose at least one of the Powerhouse activities:

⏱1 Tone n trim for tree-climbing tax collectors
(5 minutes)

What you need
• A CD/cassette player and music

What you do
Challenge the children to complete a simple two-minute routine called 'Tone n trim for tree-climbing tax collectors', to help Zacchaeus get fit. Ask them what they think they might include, but have plenty of ideas yourself. Then lead them in the workout! Reward everyone for their efforts with a visit to the **Streetwise** cafe.

⏱2 Streetwise cafe
(5–10 minutes)

What you need
• 'T' foods listed below

What you do
To link in with this session have a 'T' party. Serve food that begins with 'T', such as:
• Twirls, Topics, Toblerones or Toffee Crisps (snack sizes are available from supermarkets)
• Tomato salsa with Tangy cheese or Tortilla chips
• Tim tams or Twix biscuits
• Toast or Teacakes
• Twiglets
• Turkish delight

A great chance to sit and chat with the children and have lots of giggles over the 'T' food.
Becky, Bedford

⏱3 Unfortunately, fortunately
(5–10 minutes)

What you do
Present the following brief talk to the children:
Unfortunately, as we heard from the Bible verses, Zacchaeus was a cheat. He was probably lonely and unhappy, with no friends.
Fortunately, Zacchaeus wanted to see Jesus.

Checklist
• A 'Luke Street' sign, on display (page 19)
• The children's **Streetwise** passes, plus spare copies for newcomers
• A copy of Luke's Gospel, or a photocopy of the Bible verses on page 17 (optional)
• Materials for your choice of activities for *Open the door*, *Step inside* and *Make yourself at home*

6

6

Perhaps he knew that Jesus could change him.

Unfortunately, he couldn't see over people's heads.

Fortunately, there was a tree nearby for him to climb.

Unfortunately, he was spotted up in the tree.

Fortunately, Jesus wanted to go to his house! Jesus and Zacchaeus had a talk and Jesus forgave Zacchaeus for all the wrong things he had done. Zacchaeus changed from being a cheat to being generous. All because Jesus became his friend!

Unfortunately, there are things that we do, say and think that are wrong too.

Fortunately, Jesus wants to forgive us if we are sorry, and be our special friend. If you want to know more about how you can do that and become a friend of Jesus too, chat with *(name of appropriate person)* afterwards.

For information and help about helping children who express an interest in becoming a friend of Jesus, turn to page 12.

4 Turn the clock back
 *(10 minutes)*

What you need
- A microphone
- The questions listed below

What you do
Ask everyone to pretend that they are Zacchaeus. Move around the group with the microphone, asking different people the questions below. Explain that they should try to answer them as if they are Zacchaeus and say what they think he would have said. Choose the quiet, reticent children to answer the closed or factual questions, and the more confident, articulate children for the open questions. At any time, you could open a question up for general discussion by saying 'What does anyone else think about that?' If answers are not forthcoming, move on to another question.

1 Zacchaeus, is climbing trees a hobby of yours?
2 Why did you climb a tree the other day – was there a particular reason?
3 What happened when Jesus came to the tree?
4 What did Jesus say to you?
5 What happened next?
6 How did you feel about that?
7 How do you think the other people who were there might have felt?
8 Why do you think they would have felt like that?
9 What did you say to Jesus?

Only ask these following questions if you think

your group are ready to answer them – only you can decide for your own group.

1 Do you think Jesus changes people now?
2 Do you think Jesus loves some people more than others?
3 Some people seem to think Jesus likes very good people but other people seem to think he likes bad people? What do you think?
4 What do you think Jesus thinks about you, Zacchaeus?
5 What's it like having Jesus as a friend?

■ THOUGHTS FOR LEADERS
Don't overdo the 'Zacchaeus' problem was his height' aspect of the story, because it was clearly his behaviour with money and attitude to others that was the central issue, which changed after meeting Jesus. However, how he felt about himself and how other people reacted to him is part of the story. Children might well have had experiences of bullying and feeling unacceptable for physical reasons, which they might want to talk about. Many will relate to being an outsider. The fact that God understands and cares may be deeply significant.

5 How Jesus changed me
(5–10 minutes)

What you do
Invite a Christian friend, church member or one of your team of adult helpers to give their testimony. They could tell everyone a bit about themselves and their circumstances, when they first heard about Jesus and how he changed them and is still changing them to be more like him. Allow time for the children to ask questions, if appropriate.

6 Leaf and coin rubbings
(5 minutes)

What you need
- A variety of coins or leaves
- Pencils or wax crayons
- Thin paper

What you do
Place a piece of paper over a coin or leaf. Then rub a crayon or pencil over the paper to create a pattern. These rubbed patterns could be used as part of another activity, or stuck on the **Streetwise** pass.

07 Streetwise virtual reality
⊞ ⊙⊙ *(15–30 minutes)*

What you need
- The materials you are using to create Luke Street (see page 32)

What you do
Continue to create Luke Street. Use this activity, or 'What do you think?' to chat to the children about their experiences so far, as they work.

08 What do you think?
⊞ ⊙⊙ *(5 minutes)*

What you need
- The children's **Streetwise** passes
- Felt-tip pens or pencils

What you do
At the end of the session, encourage the children to think about what they remember most about today's programme and write or draw it in the space for The Cheat's House on the back of their **Streetwise** pass. Help any children as necessary.

Powerhouse

Choose one or both of these prayer ideas. *(5 minutes)*

Speech-bubble prayers

What you need
- A copy of the speech bubble on page 23 for each person
- A pen or pencil for each person
- A bin or bag (optional)

What you do
Give each person a blank speech bubble and a pen and invite them to put what they want to say to God on the speech bubble. With a small group, invite anyone who would like to, to read aloud what they have said as a prayer. Alternatively, invite everyone to pray their speech bubble prayer silently. Allow a few moments for this. To ensure that the private

prayers stay private, provide a bin or bag for the children to put their prayers in and then dispose of them after the session.

Coin prayers

What you need
- A money box
- A coin (plastic or real) for each person

What you do
Start by asking everyone to sit in a circle and listen to the prayer on the right as you read it. Invite them to join in with the 'Amen' at the end if they want to make it their prayer too.

Invite everyone to think of one thing that they need to change about themselves. Pass the money box around the circle. Invite each person

to post their coins in the box as a reminder of how Jesus changed Zacchaeus. As everyone does that, they could pray and ask God to change the thing they thought of, to make them more like Jesus.

'Thank you, God, that Jesus cared about Zacchaeus when no one else wanted to be his friend. Thank you for helping him to change. Help us remember that sometimes things are going on inside people that we don't know about. Help us see them as you see them, and be patient. Thank you that you love us all, whatever we are like. Amen.'

Session 7

Luke 22:8–13,19,20; 23:33,34,46; 24:1–6

Aim **To explore part of the story of the cross. Jesus took the punishment for sin and showed his power over death. That means we can know forgiveness and friendship with him for ever.**

Notes for you

As you prepare to share this story with the children, remember that for some, this may be the first time they have heard about the events surrounding Jesus' crucifixion. Through his death and resurrection Jesus conquered sin and death once and for all. Pray that the children will understand what the good news of Jesus can mean for them.

This session could be split into two, if you wanted time to develop the story of Jesus' death.

⊕ *When you see this logo, the activity is particularly appropriate for smaller groups.*

☺ *When you see this logo, the activity will also work well with older children.*

THE SECRET HOUSE

Open the door

As the children arrive, date stamp their Streetwise pass. Gather everyone together and welcome them to Streetwise. If there are newcomers, introduce them to everyone. Give out any notices at this point and mention any children who have had birthdays since your last session. Choose some or all of the activities below, according to the time you have.

▶1 Flat bread

⊕ ☺ *(10 minutes or longer!)*

What you need

- 500 g wholewheat flour, 2 g salt, 200 ml water, 30 ml melted margarine
- Bowls and spoons for mixing
- A rolling pin
- A frying pan and cooking facilities
- Blackcurrant or grape juice

What you do

As the children arrive, invite them to help you make flat bread to eat at the **Streetwise** cafe. Make sure they wash their hands, then follow these instructions:

1 Mix the flour and salt in a bowl.
2 Stir in the melted margarine.
3 Add the water a little at a time until you have a soft dough.
4 Cover the dough with a damp cloth and leave for up to an hour (half an hour will do; if you are short of time, do steps 1–4 before the session).
5 Knead the dough and divide into small balls.
6 Use the rolling pin on a floured surface to roll out each ball to about 0.5 cm thick.
7 Grease the pan and heat it on a medium heat.
8 Place the flattened dough balls in the pan one at a time. Cook each one for about 2 minutes on each side.
9 Serve at the **Streetwise** cafe with the blackcurrant or grape juice.

⑤ *The bread-making really worked! I was really surprised!* ⑤

Becky, Bedford

▶2 I remember…

⊕ ☺ *(5–10 minutes)*

What you do

Invite the children to come to the front one at a time and tell everyone about a special time in their life. It might be a birthday, a holiday or something exciting that happened to their family. Keep each contribution brief and make sure everyone who wants to say something has a turn. Ask the children what reminds them about that special time – perhaps visiting a particular place, looking at photos, or a present they were given.

You could do this activity with everyone while small groups of children make the flat bread with an adult.

▶3 Sad stories with happy endings

⊕ ☺ *(5–10 minutes)*

What you need

- Scrap paper and pencils for each group

What you do

This is played like the game known as Clumps. Divide the children into at least two groups and ask each group to sit in a circle as far away from the other groups as possible. Give the groups paper and pencils. Explain that in turn around the circle, one person from each group comes to the middle of the room. You will whisper to that person one of the Bible stories they have heard at **Streetwise**. That person returns to their group and draws the story, but is not allowed to say anything except 'Yes' or 'No'. When the group has guessed correctly, another person comes to you for the next story, then draws it, and so on. These are the stories that the groups should draw (not in their original order):

- The man let down through the roof (*The Crowded House*)
- The lady with the perfume (*The Rich House*)
- Zacchaeus meets Jesus (*The Cheat's House*)
- Jesus heals Peter's mother-in-law (*The Sick House*)
- Jesus has a meal with Martha and Mary (*The Guest House*)
- Jesus heals Jairus' daughter (*The Leader's House*)

Step inside

1 Be streetwise!
(2 minutes)

What you do
Sing the **Streetwise** song!

2 See the film
(5 minutes)

What you do
The different people in Luke Street have sad stories to tell, but they all have happy endings. This story is very sad, but it has the happiest ending of all. Watch 'The Secret House' from the **Streetwise** DVD.

3 Read the book
(3 minutes)

What you do
Ask three confident readers to stand in three different places in the room. Each one reads one of the following passages in turn as dramatically as possible: **Luke 22:8–13,19,20, Luke 23:33,34,46** and **Luke 24:1–6**. If they have a copy of the verses from page 17, the children could follow the readings.

4 Drama: At the surgery
(5–10 minutes)

What you do
If you have team members who are dramatically inclined, prepare a drama which explores the events in the Bible passages for this session. Alternatively, there is a script for you to develop at www.scriptureunion.org.uk/streetwise
Before Peter comes to ask the doctor to keep an eye on the family while he sets off with Jesus, sure all will be well. Be aware that Peter does not particularly feature in the video or the passage. Something similar with another disciple might be preferable.
After Peter returns to the doctor, convinced that Jesus is dead.
The flavour of this drama is the reverse of the others, as Peter begins with a kind of excitement, perhaps believing Jesus is about to do something amazing, ready to die if necessary, he thinks, but sure Jesus will have it all under control. In the second part, it might be appropriate for Peter to be almost 'dull' and weighed down with so much feeling. It would be possible to speak of the crucifixion here, if you chose to stick with the original passage about the Last Supper. It would be up to you how much time you spent looking at Peter's feelings and how much at the plain story. It would be possible to use Peter's uncomprehending, grieving response to explain to the children after the drama what Peter did not understand.

This session would be particularly effective with unchurched children.
Catherine, Wokingham

Make yourself at home

Choose from the following activities, making sure you include the Powerhouse prayer activity:

1 Streetwise cafe
(5–10 minutes)

What you do
If you don't do the making flat bread activity, provide some other bread for the children, such as pitta bread, bread sticks, bread rolls or even sandwiches. Serve with blackcurrant or grape juice.

The girls enjoyed reconstructing the Last Supper most of all this week.
Catherine, Wokingham

2 What Jesus' death means to me
(5–10 minutes)

What you do
Invite some people from your church to be on a panel. If possible, choose people who are known to the children. Each person in turn says briefly

Checklist
- A 'Luke Street' sign, on display (page 19)
- The children's **Streetwise** passes, plus spare copies for newcomers
- A copy of Luke's Gospel, or a photocopy of the Bible verses on page 17 for each child (optional)
- Materials for your choice of activities for *Open the door, Step inside* and *Make yourself at home*

what Jesus' death and resurrection means to them. Then encourage the panel members to ask each other questions and invite the children to ask panel members questions too. You could give the children the following questions to ask:

1 Have you ever had to keep a big secret?
2 Do you know any stories with a rescuer in them? What happens?
3 Do you get upset when you see someone you love getting hurt?
4 What would you have felt like if you had been at the party with Jesus and the next day he was killed in front of you?
5 Does the story of Jesus dying on the cross make you feel anything? If so, what?
6 What did they do to someone when they crucified them?
7 Why do you think Judas betrayed Jesus? Do you think the fact that he had been Jesus' friend makes it worse? What sort of person do you imagine Judas was?
8 The last bit of the DVD says, 'Jesus died on the cross for us'. What does this mean? Should we all have been put on a cross instead?
9 Do you think the story of the cross is a happy or sad one?

■ THOUGHTS FOR LEADERS
Give your visitors these questions in advance. Aim to create an atmosphere that is not too heavy and one where the children feel comfortable to ask their own questions. It may be that they have quite enough questions of their own without needing to rely on these! Do ensure that the panel uses child-friendly and jargon-free language and that they speak briefly.

 **Find that house!**
(5 minutes)

What you need
- 7 labels – one for each of the following houses in Luke Street – The Sick House, The Crowded House, The Rich House, The Leader's House, The Guest House, The Cheat's House and The Secret House
- Blu-Tack

What you do
Display the house labels on the walls around the room in random order. Call out the slogans below, one at a time and ask the children to run to the house in Luke Street they think it is about. For example, 'Jesus has amazing power!' refers to The Sick House where Jesus healed Peter's mother-in-law, so the children should run there. Some of these slogans could apply to more than one house.

- Jesus has amazing power! *(The Sick House)*
- Jesus can forgive sins! *(The Crowded House)*
- Jesus forgives anyone who is really sorry! *(The Rich House)*
- Nothing is impossible for Jesus! *(The Leader's House)*
- Doing what Jesus wants is best! *(The Guest House)*
- Jesus wants everyone to be his friend! *(The Cheat's House)*

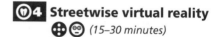 **Streetwise virtual reality**
(15–30 minutes)

What you need
- The materials you are using to create Luke Street (see page 32)

What you do
This will be the last opportunity the children have to work on Luke Street, so they will need to finish this session, ready to present it at the final session next time.

 **What do you think?**
(5 minutes)

What you need
- The children's **Streetwise** passes
- Felt-tip pens or pencils

What you do
At the end of the session, encourage the children to think about what they remember most about today's programme and write or draw it in the space for The Secret House on the back of their **Streetwise** pass. Help any children as necessary. How have the children reacted to the stories they have heard?

⊙6 Come to a celebration!
⊕ ⊚ *(5–10 minutes)*

What you need
- Paper and envelopes
- Felt-tip pens

What you do
Explain that the final session next time will be a **Streetwise** party to celebrate that Jesus is alive. Encourage the children to create invitations that can be sent to parents, friends and church members, inviting them to **Streetwise** to join the party.

Why not make Easter cards too, using ideas from this session? The children could give them out with the invitations or at the celebration. If Easter is not for some months, you could keep the cards and, shortly before Easter, send each child their card, as a reminder of **Streetwise**.

ⓖ *Several children addressed their invitations to children who had not been for a few weeks, saying they thought they would enjoy it. We hadn't asked them to do this.* Ⓢ
Becky, Bedford

Powerhouse

Include one or both of these prayer activities in your session. *(5 minutes)*

Thought bubble prayers
⊕ ⊚

What you need
- A photocopy of the thought bubble on page 23 for each person
- A felt-tip pen or pencil for each person

What you do
Give everyone a copy of the thought bubble and a pen or pencil. Invite them to think what they would like to put in their thought bubble to complete the phrase: 'Jesus, I think

you are…'. Make sure adult helpers are available to act as scribes for any children who need help. After a couple of minutes, invite each person to read what they have written as a prayer, either aloud in turn, or silently.

Cross-legged prayers

What you need
- Recording of a children's song about the cross, such as 'When I think about the cross' (*kidsource* 376) or 'Jesus, thank you for the cross' (*kidsource* 214)
- CD/cassette player

What you do
Sit four children cross-legged back to back, to form the central part of a cross shape. Ask some more children to sit cross-legged in the shape of the arms of the cross and the rest to make up the length of the cross and the section above the cross-piece. Ask them to put their hands in a cross shape, then ask each child to close their eyes and picture Jesus on the cross. Play one of the songs about the cross and let this be each child's prayer to God.

Session 8

**Luke
24:13–43**

Aim **To rejoice that Jesus came alive! He is alive today and we can know him.**

THE COUNTRY HOUSE

Notes for you

Pray that as the children celebrate the resurrection, they will understand that Jesus is alive today and wants to be their special friend for ever.

This final session in the series celebrates the resurrection of Jesus with a **Streetwise** street party to which parents, friends and church members are invited! Make sure that anyone who has helped with **Streetwise** in any way receives a special invitation. It would be good to have one or two church leaders there. It's also a good opportunity to recap on what everyone has learned about Jesus during the **Streetwise** series.

 When you see this logo, the activity is particularly appropriate for smaller groups.

 When you see this logo, the activity will also work well with older children.

Open the door

If possible, decorate the room in advance with balloons and streamers. Play background music as the children arrive to create a celebratory atmosphere. As the children arrive, date stamp their Streetwise pass. Gather everyone together and welcome them to Streetwise, adding a special welcome to visitors. Give out any notices at this point and mention any children who have had birthdays since your last session. Choose some or all of the activities below, according to the time you have.

◑1 Streetwise cafe
 (Throughout the session)

What you need
• Tea and coffee for visitors (optional)

What you do
Invite any visitors to **Streetwise** to sit in the **Streetwise** cafe area and if possible, serve them tea or coffee. Invite them to relax and watch what the children have been up to!

◑2 Bunting bonanza
(5 minutes)

What you need
• A4 paper folded diagonally and cut into triangles
• Pencils and crayons or felt-tip pens
• A roll of string and sticky tape

What you do
As the children arrive, invite them to design a **Streetwise** flag to create bunting for the street party. They need to draw something they have learned about at **Streetwise**, so it could be a house Jesus visited, or one of the people who met Jesus. As each flag is finished, attach it to the string with sticky tape. Display the string of bunting across the room.

◑3 Old favourites
 (10–15 minutes)

What you do
Choose some activities from the last seven sessions of *Open the door* and do them again. Select ones that the children have particularly enjoyed. Alternatively, ask the children to choose from a selection that you have prepared. Explain to the visitors what the children are doing and what they have been learning about at **Streetwise**.

◑4 Streetwise virtual reality
 (5 minutes)

What you do
Depending on how you did this activity, invite the children to show the visitors what they created for 'Streetwise virtual reality'. If appropriate, they could explain what happened at each of the houses.

🄶*As it's Christmas-time, Streetwise is taking a detour to Bethlehem! We are creating another house in Bethlehem.*🄶

Sue, Yate

Step inside

1 Be streetwise!
 *(5 minutes)*

What you do
Sing the **Streetwise** song! Get the children to teach the song to the visitors!

2 See the film
(5 minutes)

What you do
Have you ever met someone you know who didn't recognise you, or maybe you didn't recognise them? That's what happened to some of Jesus' friends when they were walking home one evening… Show 'The Country House' from the **Streetwise** DVD.

3 Read the book
(5–10 minutes)

What you need
• A photocopy of the verses from page 18 for each person
• A felt-tip pen for each person

What you do
You will need to rehearse this in advance. Choose four confident readers to present **Luke 24:13–43**. One reads the narrative, while the others take the parts of Cleopas, his friend and Jesus. Alternatively, one person can read all the verses while the other three people mime. You may prefer to omit verses 19–24 to keep the reading a bit shorter.

If they have a copy of the verses, give each child a felt-tip pen and invite them to complete the following tasks. Give a few clues if the children are stuck. Make sure one or two adult helpers are available to offer assistance if necessary.

1 Draw a line under the words that tell us that Jesus' friends didn't recognise him. (verse 16)
2 Circle the number of kilometres that the friends had to walk home. (verse 13)
3 Draw faces beside the text to show how the two friends looked. (verse 17)
4 Draw how the two men looked when they realised that it was Jesus with them. (verses 31 and 32)

5 Draw a signpost and write on it how far the men walked (or ran) to get back to Jerusalem to tell the others that they had seen Jesus. (11 kilometres – about 7 miles!)
6 Put ticks beside things which you think are good news.
7 Put a question mark beside anything you don't understand and talk to an adult about it.
8 In the space at the bottom of the page, write 'Jesus is …' and add the word 'alive' in really big letters. Then, add any other words that describe what you think about Jesus and all the things he did in Luke Street.

4 Drama: At the surgery
(5–10 minutes)

What you do
If you have team members who are dramatically inclined, prepare a drama in advance which explores what happened after Jesus' resurrection.

Alternatively, there is a script to develop at www.scriptureunion.org.uk/streetwise
One session only The doctor is visiting Jerusalem and Peter has recommended him to a friend, Cleopas, who has foot problems after walking 11 kilometres to Emmaus, and back. Cleopas then tells the doctor about what happened to him on the way there. Three people are required, unless you wanted to send the disciple on Peter's recommendation without Peter himself.

Checklist
• A 'Luke Street' sign, on display (page 19)
• The completed Luke Street on display (if you did '**Streetwise** virtual reality')
• The children's **Streetwise** passes, ready to check and date stamp as they arrive, plus spare copies for newcomers
• Decorations to create a party atmosphere, such as balloons, streamers and party hats
• A copy of Luke's Gospel, or a photocopy of the Bible verses on page 18 for each child (optional)
• Materials for your choice of activities for *Open the door*, *Step inside* and *Make yourself at home*

8

8

Make yourself at home

Choose from the following activities, making sure you include the Powerhouse prayer activity:

We didn't choose too many activities because of the good number of unchurched parents. We wanted time to talk together.
Becky, Bedford

1 Streetwise highlights
(10–15 minutes)

What you do
Choose *Make yourself at home* activities from the other sessions that were popular with the children. Repeat them and talk about which house in Luke Street they relate to. Ask the children to tell everyone what happened when Jesus visited those houses.

We gave each child a name of one of Jesus' disciples or someone who had appeared in Streetwise. When the name of that person was called out, the children had to run round two chairs and back to their place... And when 'Streetwise' was called, everyone ran! Not a good idea for big groups though!
Dougie, Evesham

2 Pass the Parcel
(5 minutes)

What you need
A parcel with several layers and a small prize in the middle. Put one of the following questions in each layer (you could make up your own, if you wish):

1 What is your favourite food?
2 Would you rather eat a giant pizza or a bucket of spaghetti?
3 Where would your ideal holiday be?
4 If you could play any musical instrument you liked, what would it be?
5 Which is your favourite house in Luke Street and why?
6 What was the best thing you learned about Jesus?

7 What did you learn about Jesus that was surprising?
8 Which game or activity have you enjoyed most at **Streetwise**?

What you do
Play Pass the Parcel in the normal way, but when a child unwraps a layer, they should try to answer the question which has been hidden in that layer. If a child has difficulty answering, ask the others to help out. Don't let it become pressurised or competitive!

3 'Jesus is alive' twizzler
(10 minutes)

What you need
• Photocopy of the twizzler template from page 24 copied onto card (one per child)
• A pencil or dowel per child
• Sticky tape

What you do
Colour in Jesus, but not the door. Fold the card in half and open it out again, then stick a pencil or piece of dowel to the back of the door. Fold the Jesus half over the top and stick down. When the children twizzle the pencil between their fingers, it looks as though Jesus appears in front of the locked door.

4 What do you think?
(5 minutes)

What you need
• The children's **Streetwise** passes
• Felt-tip pens or pencils

What you do
At the end of the session, encourage the children to think about what they remember most about today's programme and write or draw it in the space for The Country House on the back of their **Streetwise** pass. Help any children as necessary. If appropriate, encourage the children to explain what they have written on their pass with their parents/carers.

Make sure that you have informed parents, carers and the children of your regular children's programme and any plans you have to run another programme like **Streetwise**.

 **Streetwise cafe**
 (5–10 minutes)

What you need
• Party food for everyone

What you do
Finish the **Streetwise** party by serving the party food. Encourage the children and adult helpers to mix with the visitors. Play Christian music quietly in the background.Give any notices and invite the children and their parents to other church activities. Remember to thank all the people who have contributed to **Streetwise**, especially those who have worked behind the scenes. Then relax and enjoy the celebrations!

Powerhouse

Include this activity in your programme. *(10 minutes)*

Graffiti wall

What you need
• A large sheet of paper
• Sticky tape
• A felt-tip pen or pencil for each person

What you do
Stick the large sheet of paper on the wall where it is easily accessible to write on. Invite everyone who wants to (visitors included) to take it in turns to write a 'graffiti' prayer of praise or thanks to God. Encourage the children to think about all the different things that Jesus did in **Streetwise** and what they learned about him.

When everyone has finished, read some or all of the prayers aloud, pausing after each one. Invite everyone to join in with a loud 'Amen' at the end, to show that they agree with what has been prayed.

Books
to help you

Jesus and the cheat
Diane Walker

The story of Zacchaeus is beautifully retold in *Jesus and the cheat*. It is available in two formats, a big book for group use and a child's reader.

Big Book: £19.99, 1 85999 722 8
Child's reader: £3.50, 1 85999 723 6

Others in the series include:
Jesus puts things right, *Jesus and the starving crowd* and *Jesus and the breakfast barbecue*

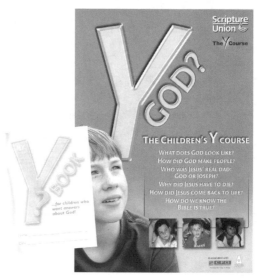

Y God?
Steve Hutchinson

Y God? is the children's Y course and is ideal for children who are investigating the Christian faith. Six sessions use questions asked by children about Christianity and seek to answer them in child-friendly terms.

Pack: £9.99, 1 85999 552 7
My Y book (pack of 10): £6.00, 1 85999 687 6

See page 12 for details of Scripture Union's range of booklets about the Christian faith.

Children Finding Faith
Francis Bridger

How can we help children know God? In this prize-winning book, Francis Bridger explores how children develop in their faith.
£6.99, 1 85999 323 0

Holiday club material

Xpedition Force

Doug Swanney

A 5-day holiday programme, based on the week leading up to Jesus' crucifixion and resurrection, using Matthew's Gospel.

Resource book: £8.99, 1 85999 685 X

DVD: £19.99, 1 84427 035 1

Matthew's Story (SIngle Gospel): £1.99, 1 84427 034 3

Matthew's Story (10-pack): £10,00, 1 84427 033 5

Envelope (contains two resource books, DVD and one Matthew's Story): £34.99, 1 84427 037 8

Promotional material is available from CPO.

To order these or any of Scripture Union's products, visit your local Christian bookshp or contact SU Mail Order:

Scripture Union Mail Order
PO Box 5148
Milton Keynes MLO
MK2 2YX
Tel: 0845 07 06 006 Fax: 01908 856020
Web: www.scriptureunion.org.uk

Seaside Rock

Dave Godfrey

This 5-day programme follows Peter as he encounters Jesus.

Resource book (with CD of the Seaside Rock song and memory verse songs): £9.99, 1 85999 567 5

Video: £19.99, 1 85999 681 7

Postcards (50-pack, 10 cards per session): £10.00, 1 85999 699 X

eye level clubs...

- are for boys and girls aged 5 to 11.
- are for children who are not yet part of a church (as well as those who are).
- don't assume that children know much about Jesus or have had any experience of church.
- recognise that all children are open to God and the wonder of his world, and that all children can have valid spiritual experiences, regardless of church background.
- aim to give children one of the best hours in their week.
- provide opportunities for appropriate and respectful relationships between children and adults, working in small groups.
- plan to introduce children to the Bible in ways that allow for imagination, exploration and learning difficulties.
- are led by those who long to see children become lifelong followers of Jesus Christ.
- are led by those who will put themselves at a child's level, so that together they can catch sight of Jesus.

Find out about other eye level clubs and contribute to the development of thinking on reaching children who are beyond the church by registering your club at www.scriptureunion.org.uk/streetwise
Your involvement is needed!